FHG

50
Bed &
Breakfasts
in Britain

For holidaymakers & business travellers

Overnight Stops & Short Breaks

Pubs & Inns

Pet-friendly accommodation

2013

Double-Gate Farm
near Wells, Somerset

Fisherman's Return
Winterton-on-Sea, Norfolk

www.holidayguides.com

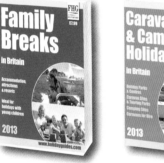

Contents

SOUTH WEST ENGLAND

5

Cornwall, Devon,
Dorset, Gloucestershire,
Somerset, Wiltshire

©MAPS IN MINUTES™ (2011)
Contains Ordnance Survey data
©Crown Copyright
and database right 2010

LONDON & SOUTH EAST ENGLAND

76

London, Berkshire,
Buckinghamshire, Hampshire,
Isle of Wight, Kent, Oxfordshire,
Surrey, East Sussex, West Sussex

EAST OF ENGLAND

107

Cambridgeshire,
Essex, Hertfordshire,
Norfolk, Suffolk

EAST MIDLANDS

121

Derbyshire, Leicestershire & Rutland,
Lincolnshire, Northamptonshire,
Nottinghamshire

HEART OF ENGLAND

134

Herefordshire, Shropshire,
Staffordshire, Warwickshire,
West Midlands, Worcestershire

YORKSHIRE

148

East Yorkshire, North Yorkshire,
South Yorkshire, West Yorkshire

NORTH EAST ENGLAND

174

Durham, Northumberland

NORTH WEST ENGLAND

187

Cheshire, Cumbria, Lancashire

WALES

Anglesey & Gwynedd	213
North Wales	216
Carmarthenshire	218
Ceredigion	218
Pembrokeshire	219
Powys	221
South Wales	223

SCOTLAND

Aberdeen, Banff & Moray	226
Argyll & Bute	228
Ayrshire & Arran	235
Borders	239
Dumfries & Galloway	245
Edinburgh & Lothians	248
Glasgow & District	251
Highlands	252
Lanarkshire	266
Perth & Kinross	267
Stirling & The Trossachs	268
Scottish Islands	270

Pubs & Inns	272
Pet-Friendly Accommodation	276
Website Directory	281
Readers' Offer Vouchers	289
Index of Towns & Counties	301

England and Wales • Counties

1. Plymouth	12. Windsor & Maidenhead	23. Milton Keynes	34. Blackpool
2. Torbay	13. Bracknell Forest	24. Peterborough	35. N.E. Lincolnshire
3. Poole	14. Wokingham	25. Leicester	36. North Lincolnshire
4. Bournemouth	15. Reading	26. Nottingham	37. Kingston-upon-Hull
5. Southampton	16. West Berkshire	27. Derby	38. York
6. Portsmouth	17. Swindon	28. Telford & Wrekin	39. Redcar & Cleveland
7. Brighton & Hove	18. Bath & Northeast Somerset	29. Stoke-on-Trent	40. Middlesborough
8. Medway	19. North Somerset	30. Warrington	41. Stockton-on-Tees
9. Thurrock	20. Bristol	31. Halton	42. Darlington
10. Southend	21. South Gloucestershire	32. Merseyside	43. Hartlepool
11. Slough	22. Luton	33. Blackburn with Darwen	

NORTH WALES
a. Denbighshire
b. Flintshire
c. Wrexham

SOUTH WALES
d. Swansea
e. Neath & Port Talbot
f. Bridgend
g. Rhondda Cynon Taff
h. Merthyr Tydfil
i. Vale of Glamorgan
j. Cardiff
k. Caerphilly
l. Blaenau Gwent
m. Torfaen
n. Newport
o. Monmouthshire

©MAPS IN MINUTES™ (2011) Contains Ordnance Survey data ©Crown Copyright and database right 2010

Cornwall

Bude

Mawgan Porth

SB
Wi-Fi

• Bake Farm •

Pelynt, Looe, Cornwall PL13 2QQ
Tel: 01503 220244

SB

This is an old farmhouse, bearing the Trelawney Coat of Arms (1610), situated midway between Looe and Fowey. Two double and one triple bedroom, all en suite and decorated to a high standard, have tea/coffee making facilities and TV. Sorry, no pets, no smoking. Open from March to October. A car is essential for touring the area, ample parking. There is much to see and do here – horse riding, coastal walks, golf, National Trust properties, the Eden Project and Heligan Gardens are within easy reach. The sea is only five miles away and there is shark fishing at Looe.

Bed and Breakfast from £32 to £35. Brochure available on request.

e-mail: bakefarm@btopenworld.com • www.bakefarm.co.uk

BRE-PEN FARM

**Mawgan Porth
Cornwall
TR8 4AL**

SB

Wi-Fi

A warm Cornish welcome awaits you from Rod and Jill in a friendly farmhouse on a working farm. The National Trust Coastal Path skirts the farm, making it an ideal walking area. The beaches of Mawgan Porth and Watergate Bay are within easy walking distance, both ideal for surfing. A short drive east takes you to the historic fishing port of Padstow, Bedruthan Steps and many glorious sandy beaches. Ideally situated for visiting the many attractions of Cornwall.

Double/Twin en suite rooms £35.00 pppn, Family suite £97.50. All with tea/coffee facilities and colour TV. Traditional farmhouse breakfast; vegetarians catered for. Holistic therapies available: Reflexology, Massage and Indian Head Massage. Free WiFi.

Rod & Jill Brake, Bre-Pen Farm,
Mawgan Porth, Newquay TR8 4AL
Tel: 01637 860420 • www.bre-penfarm.co.uk
e-mail: jill.brake@virgin.net

TREWITHEN FARMHOUSE is a renovated Cornish Roundhouse, set in a large garden and situated on a working farm enjoying country and coastal views. The picturesque town of Padstow with its pretty harbour and narrow streets with famous fish restaurants is only three miles away. St Merryn Parish boasts seven beautiful sandy beaches and bays. Also coastal walks, golf, fishing and horse riding on neighbouring farm. Hire a bike or walk along the Camel Trail cycle and footpath - winding for 18 miles along the River Camel. Eden Project 20 miles.

SB

Wi-Fi

The accommodation has been tastefully decorated to complement the exposed beams and original features. All bedrooms are en suite with hairdryers, clocks, TVs and hot drink facilities.

**Mrs Sandra May,
Trewithen Farm, St Merryn,
Near Padstow PL28 8JZ**
01841 520420 • 07709 635999
www.trewithenfarmhouse.com

• Parking • Full English breakfast • TV lounge.
• Bed and Breakfast from £40 per person per night.
• Winter breaks available. • Non-smoking.

e-mail: maystrewithen@aol.com

Newquay

SB

Wi-Fi

Wi-Fi

Seaways

Seaways is a small family-run guest house, 250 yards from a safe, sandy beach. Surfing, riding, sailing, tennis, squash, golf, and lovely cliff walks nearby. Polzeath is the ideal base for exploring all that North Cornwall has to offer. Padstow is a short distance by ferry; other places of interest include Tintagel, Boscastle and Port Isaac.

All bedrooms with en suite or private bathrooms - two double, one twin and a single room • Sittingroom; dining room • Children welcome (reduced price for under 10s) • Cot, high chair available. Comfortable family holiday assured with plenty of good home cooking.

Also available: self-catering annexe, sleeps 4. For details see
www.crwholidays.co.uk (Ref RK23)

Non-smoking establishment.
Open all year round.
Bed and Breakfast £40pppn.

Mrs P. White, Seaways, Polzeath PL27 6SU
Tel: 01208 862382
e-mail: pauline@seaways99.freeserve.co.uk
www.seaways-polzeath.co.uk

This small, detached, family-run Victorian hotel stands in the heart of the picturesque village of St Agnes, convenient for many outstanding country and coastal walks. Set in mature gardens we can offer peace and relaxation after the beach, which is approximately half-a-mile away. Accommodation is provided in generous sized rooms, mostly en suite and all with colour TV. Public rooms comprise lounge, bar, dining rooms. Private parking.

Wi-Fi

Cleaderscroft Hotel

16 British Road, St Agnes TR5 0TZ

Tel: 01872 552349 • Ted & Jeanie Ellis

- B&B from £36pppn (sharing).
- Non-smoking • Regret no pets
- Self-catering annexe available

e-mail: tedellis@cchotel.fsnet.co.uk

www.cchotel.fsnet.co.uk

CORNERWAYS GUEST HOUSE

SB

Centrally situated, and ideal for touring both the North and South Coasts of Cornwall. Ideal for rambling and walking holidays, and for visiting many nearby tourist attractions such as The Eden Project, or the Leisure centre in St Austell, with full size pool, squash courts and fitness centre.

There is a choice of double, twin or single bedrooms, some of which are en suite; ironing board, iron and hairdryer available.

Full English or Continental Breakfast offered and Bed and Breakfast prices start from £22.

**Penwinnick Road
St Austell
Cornwall PL25 5DS
Tel: Bookings 01726 61579
Visitors: 01726 71874
Fax: 01726 66871**

St Austell, Truro

SB

Polgreen is a family-run dairy farm nestling in the Pentewan Valley in an Area of Outstanding Natural Beauty. One mile from the coast and four miles from the picturesque fishing village of Mevagissey, a perfect location for a relaxing holiday in the glorious Cornish countryside.

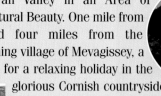

Centrally situated, Polgreen is ideally placed for touring all of Cornwall's many attractions; Cornish Way Leisure Trail adjoining farm. Within a few minutes' drive of the spectacular Eden Project and Heligan Gardens. All rooms with private facilities, colour TV, tea/coffee making facilities. Guest lounge. Children welcome.

Terms from £30 per person per night.

Mrs Liz Berryman, Polgreen Farm, London Apprentice, St Austell PL26 7AP • Tel: 01726 75151

e-mail: polgreen.farm@btinternet.com

www.polgreenfarm.co.uk

AA
★★★★
Guest Accommodation

SB

Wi-Fi

TRENONA FARM

Ruan High Lanes, Truro, Cornwall TR2 5JS

Enjoy a relaxing stay on this mixed farm, on the unspoilt Roseland Peninsula midway

between Truro and St Austell (home of the Eden Project). Victorian farmhouse with four guest bedrooms, all of which are double/family rooms with colour TV, mini-fridge, tea/coffee making facilities, with either en suite or private bathroom. Separate TV lounge and dining room, together with gardens and a patio. Brochure available.

Children welcome • Pets welcome by arrangement.

www.trenonafarmholidays.co.uk

Tel: 01872 501339

enquiries@trenonafarmholidays.co.uk   Open March to November

Wadebridge

Pengelly Farmhouse

SB

A Listed Georgian farmhouse on a working dairy farm, in a quiet location overlooking wooded valleys. Tastefully decorated and centrally heated throughout, offering one double and one twin room, both en suite, with TV, radio, hairdryer and beverage tray. Full English breakfast, using mainly local produce, is served in the traditional-style diningroom. Special diets by prior arrangement. Comfortable lounge with TV/video. Large garden with outstanding views for relaxing.
B&B from £26. Static caravan also available.

Mrs E. Hodge, Pengelly Farm, Burlawn, Wadebridge PL27 7LA
Tel: 01208 814217 • e-mail: hodgepete@hotmail.com

www.pengellyfarm.co.uk

An ideal walking, touring and cycling base, only six miles from the coast, with sailing, surfing, golf, riding and coastal walks; Camel Trail, the Saints' Way and Pencarrow House nearby. The Eden Project 35 minutes' drive, Padstow 20 minutes, Wadebridge 1½ miles, with shopping, pubs, restaurants, leisure facilities.

Barnstaple

Devon

SB

Lower Yelland Farm Guest House

Situated half way between Barnstaple and Bideford, this delightfully modernised 17thC farmhouse accommodation is part of a working farm. The farm is centrally located for easy access to the many attractions of North Devon, its beautiful beaches, varied walks and sports facilities including golf, surfing, fishing, riding etc. Its proximity to both Exmoor and Dartmoor makes this location perfect for those who wish to explore. Instow with its sandy beach, pubs and restaurants is a just mile away. It lies adjacent to the Tarka Trail, part of the South West Coastal Footpath, and RSPB bird sanctuary.

The bed and breakfast accommodation comprises 2 twin/super king-size and one room with four-poster bed, 2 double rooms and 2 single rooms; all rooms en suite, with TV and tea/coffee making facilities. Breakfast includes eggs from our free-range chickens, home-made bread, jams and marmalade. The delightful sitting room has a large selection of books for those who want to relax and browse.

AA
★★★★
Guest
Accommodation

Winner Golden
Achievement Award of
Excellence for Devon
Retreat of the Year

Please visit our website for further details

www.loweryellandfarm.co.uk

Lower Yelland Farm Guest House, Fremington, Barnstaple EX31 3EN
Tel: 01271 860101 • e-mail: peterday@loweryellandfarm.co.uk

Think of Devon, and wild moorland springs to mind, but this is a county of contrasts, with the wild moors of the Exmoor National Park to the north fringed by dramatic cliffs and combes, golden beaches and picturesque harbours, and busy market towns and sleepy villages near the coast. An experience not to be missed is the cliff railway between the pretty little port of Lynmouth and its twin village of Lynton high on the cliff, with a backdrop of dramatic gorges or combes. In the centre of the county lies Dartmoor, with its vast open spaces, granite tors and spectacular moorland, rich in wildlife and ideal for walking, pony trekking and cycling. The Channel coast to the south, with its gentle climate and scenery, is an attractive destination at any time of year.

Bideford

West Titchberry Farm

SB

Situated on the rugged North Devon coast, West Titchberry is a working traditionally-run stock farm, half a mile from Hartland Point.

The South West Coastal Path skirts around the farm making it an ideal base for walkers.

Pick ups and kit transfers available. Long term parking on site.

The three guest rooms comprise an en suite family room; one double and one twin room, with washbasins.

Bathroom/toilet and separate shower room on the same floor plus a downstairs toilet. All bedrooms have colour TV, radio, hairdryer, tea/coffee making facilities. Outside, guests may take advantage of a sheltered walled garden. Sorry, no pets. Nearest accommodation to heliport for winter departures for Lundy Island

Hartland village is 3 miles away, Clovelly 6 miles, Bideford and Westward Ho! 16 miles and Bude 18 miles.

- *B&B from £27.50–£32 pppn (based on 2 sharing)*
- *2 Course Evening meal £13 (please book)*
- *Children welcome at reduced rates for under 11s*
- *Open all year except Christmas*
- *Welcome tray on arrival*

Mrs Yvonne Heard, West Titchberry Farm, Hartland Point, Near Bideford EX39 6AU

Tel & Fax: 01237 441287

Bradford, Dartmoor

DEVONCOURT HOTEL
& APARTMENTS

Standing in four acres of mature subtropical gardens, overlooking two miles of sandy beach, yet within easy reach of Dartmoor and Exeter, Devoncourt provides an ideal base for a family holiday at any time of year.

ACCOMMODATION: comprises luxury en suite bedrooms (single, double/twin and family), all with tea/coffee making and TV/DVD. In addition there are one and two bedroom self-catering apartments, with excellent furnishings and well-equipped kitchenettes; many with sea views/balconies.

AMENITIES: include swimming pool, sauna, steam room, whirlpool spa, solarium and fitness centre, snooker room, hair salon.

OUT OF DOORS: tennis court, croquet lawn, attractive outdoor heated pool, 18-hole putting green, all within the grounds.

OUTLOOK: palm trees and uninterrupted sea views of the Bay form a Continental landscape to this first-class hotel in the delightful Devon resort of Exmouth.

RESTAURANT: Brasserie 16, overlooking the gardens and coastline, offers a friendly welcome, good food and good service.

DEVONCOURT HOTEL
& APARTMENTS
Douglas Avenue, Exmouth, Devon EX8 2EX
Tel: 01395 272277
e-mail: enquiries@devoncourt.com • www.devoncourthotel.com

Honiton, Ilfracombe

SB

Wi-Fi

As far away from stress as it is possible to be!

Odle Farm

We have three Bed and Breakfast rooms. Our double room has an en suite bathroom and views across the valley; the twin-bedded room has an en suite shower room and views over the courtyard and gardens. Our family suite consists of a double room, a twin room and a private bathroom. All rooms have a TV and tea and coffee making facilities. You are welcome to use the lounge downstairs during your stay which has a TV with DVD and Freeview. Your full English breakfast using local produce and our own free-range eggs is served in our conservatory, which has amazing views of the Otter Valley.

No pets • Non-smoking

There is a cosy pub in the village of Upottery and several other excellent hostelries in the vicinity. Odle Farm provides a convenient stop if you are passing through Devon or an ideal base for a short break. B&B £32.50-£45.00pp,

Odle Farm, New Road, Upottery, Near Honiton EX14 9QE
Tel: 01404 861105 • www.odlefarm.co.uk • email: info@odlefarm.co.uk

SB

Wi-Fi

WENTWORTH HOUSE

Wentworth House, a friendly, family-run private hotel built as a gentleman's residence in 1857, standing in lovely gardens only a stone's throw from the town and minutes from the sea, harbour and Torrs Walks.

En suite rooms with colour TV and tea/coffee making facilities. Family rooms sleeping up to four persons. Home-cooked food with packed lunches on request.

Spacious bar/ lounge.
Secure storage for bicycles etc. Private parking in grounds.
Open all year. No smoking.

Bed & Breakfast from £24.00 • Evening Meal £14.00 per person.
Discounted rates for bookings of 3 nights or more.

Stay a few days or a week, Geoff & Sharon will make your visit a pleasant one.

2 Belmont Road, Ilfracombe EX34 8DR • Tel & Fax: 01271 863048
e-mail: wentworthhouse@tiscali.co.uk • www.hotelilfracombe.co.uk

Ilfracombe

Ilfracombe, Kingsbridge

SB
Licensed

Wi-Fi

VARLEY HOUSE • Chambercombe Park, Ilfracombe EX34 9QW

Tel: 01271 863927 • Fax: 01271 879299 • e-mail: info@varleyhouse.co.uk • www.varleyhouse.co.uk

Built at the turn of the 20th century for returning officers from the Boer War, Varley House generates a feeling of warmth and relaxation, combined with an enviable position overlooking Hillsborough Nature Reserve. Winding paths lead to the Harbour and several secluded coves. Our attractive, spacious, fully en suite bedrooms all have colour TV, central heating, generous beverage tray, hairdryer and clock radio alarm.

Superb food, beautiful surroundings and that special friendly atmosphere so essential to a relaxing holiday. Cosy separate bar. Car park. Children over 5 years of age. Dogs by arrangement. NON-SMOKING. *Bed and Breakfast from £30pp. Weekly from £189pp. Low season 3 day breaks from £80pp.*

MARSH MILLS

Marsh Mills is in the heart of the beautiful South Hams countryside. Four miles from Kingsbridge, 17 miles east of Plymouth, we are at the end of a quiet lane just off the A379. Bigbury Bay 4 miles, Dartmoor 8 miles. A former Mill House, now a smallholding with friendly animals, we have several acres of gardens, orchard and pastures. Family-run, a warm welcome is extended to all our guests.

Our two en suite bedrooms have tea/coffee making facilities, satellite TV, room heaters and are comfortably furnished. Car parking.

Bed & Breakfast from £31pppn.

Mrs M. Newsham, Marsh Mills, Aveton Gifford, Kingsbridge, South Devon TQ7 4JW
Tel: 01548 550549 • www.Marshmills.co.uk
e-mail: Newsham@Marshmills.co.uk
jrm@Newsham.eclipse.co.uk

symbols 🐎🐴SB♿️♀️Wi-Fi

🐕	*Pets Welcome*	🐎	*Children Welcome*
SB	*Short Breaks*	♿️	*Suitable for Disabled Guests*
♀️	*Licensed*	Wi-Fi	*Wi-Fi available*

Lynmouth

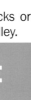

Lynmouth/Lynton

The North Cliff Hotel, standing in its own grounds, has some of the finest views of the North Devon coastline. It is in a peaceful position some 500 feet above sea level overlooking Lynmouth Bay, and a 200 metre walk to Lynton. With car parking facilities on the forecourt, the hotel is an ideal base for exploring the coastline and Exmoor National Park, whether it is your annual holiday or off-season break.

The rooms boast some of the best sea views in Lynton; bedrooms are individually decorated and are en suite. All bedrooms have colour television and facilities for making your favourite beverage.

We can accommodate family gatherings or walking parties as there are 7 doubles, 2 twins, 1 single and 4 family rooms (which can be used as twins or doubles).

We have a licensed bar available for a drink after a hard day of walking or an aperitif before dinner in our restaurant, which has magnificent sea and coastal views.

Children of all ages and pets are very welcome.

Local activities include walking, riding, tennis, and putting. The famous water-powered Cliff Railway linking Lynton and Lynmouth passes within a few feet of the hotel and is accessed via the stepped garden.

North Cliff Hotel
North Walk, Lynton, North Devon EX35 6HJ

Tel: 01598 752357
e-mail: holidays@northcliffhotel.co.uk
www.northcliffhotel.co.uk

SB

Wi-Fi

Moorlands

**Woody Bay, Parracombe
Devon EX31 4RA
01598 763224**

SB

Moorlands, formerly the
Woody Bay Station Hotel, is a
family-run Guesthouse in a most
beautiful part of North Devon –
*where countryside and
comfort combine.*

Very comfortable and quiet single, double or family suite accommodation,
all en suite with bath or shower. Moorlands has a licensed dining room
and residents' lounge with open fire. Set in extensive gardens.
A perfect retreat for the country lover to relax and unwind.

*Bed and Breakfast £42.00pppn,
with discounts for longer stays.
Some ground floor rooms and
self-catering apartments available.
Please see our website for special offers.*

www.moorlandshotel.co.uk

River Lyn View

26 Watersmeet Road, Lynmouth EX35 6EP
01598 753501 • www.riverlynview.com
Well presented en suite bedrooms with TV and tea/coffee facilities.
A full English breakfast is served in the cosy dining area.
Comfortable lounge. Pets welcome. Exmoor National Park and
other places of interest are a short drive away.

SB

Wi-Fi

Great Sloncombe Farm
Moretonhampstead Devon TQ13 8QF
Tel: 01647 440595

Share the magic of Dartmoor all year round while staying in our lovely
13th century farmhouse full of interesting historical features. A working
mixed farm set amongst peaceful meadows and woodland abundant in
wild flowers and animals, including badgers, foxes, deer and buzzards.
A welcoming and informal place to relax and explore the moors and
Devon countryside. Comfortable double and twin rooms with en suite
facilities, TV, central heating and coffee/tea making facilities. Delicious
Devonshire breakfasts with new baked bread.

Open all year~No smoking~Farm Stay UK
e-mail: hmerchant@sloncombe.freeserve.co.uk • www.greatsloncombefarm.co.uk

AA
★★★★
FARMHOUSE

PARSONAGE FARM

Wi-Fi

A warm welcome awaits you at our family-run organic farm, situated approximately one mile from the picturesque village of Iddesleigh where there is an excellent 15th century inn called the Duke of York. The ancient market town of Hatherleigh is three miles away and has a weekly market and auction. The Tarka Trail passes through our farmyard, and 400m of salmon trout fishing is available on the farm boundary, where there is a fishing hut, a secluded spot for a picnic (chairs and table provided.) There are other walks around the farm with an abundance of wildlife and flowers and a chance to watch the cows being milked from a gallery. RHS Rosemoor is about 8 miles away and the nearest surfing beaches are on the North Devon and North Cornwall coast, all within easy reach. An ideal peaceful haven for touring both Devon and Cornwall, including Dartmoor and Exmoor.

Our farm and surrounding area was the basis of Michael Morpurgo's book "War Horse" which was turned into a play in the West End, and then made into a film by Steven Spielberg. We have recently converted our 15thC old cob barn into a museum based on "War Horse" and World War 1 (www.warhorsevalley.co.uk) Another book by Michael Morpurgo, called "Private Peaceful", is also based on WW1.

Accommodation consists of a two-bedroom family room en suite and a double room en suite, both with tea/coffee making facilities, central heating, digital TV and WiFi. There is a games room with table tennis, darts, snooker or pool. Open Easter – October. No smoking and no pets.

B&B from £34pp for double room, £38pp for single room. Reduction for weekly bookings and children.

Mrs Rosemary Ward, Parsonage Farm, Iddesleigh, Winkleigh, Devon EX19 8SN
Tel: 01837 810318 • e-mail: roseward01@yahoo.co.uk
www.devon-holiday.com/parsonage

Peace and Tranquillity are easily found at

SB

A delightful 16th century Devon longhouse in the beautiful Otter Valley

Fluxton Farm

Occupying a sheltered position just south of Ottery St Mary, and only 4 miles from the sea at Sidmouth. We are no longer a working farm, but keep ducks and chickens and have lots of cats. We have 7 bedrooms, all en suite, and two charming sitting rooms. Our beamed dining room has a large open fireplace and separate tables, where a full English breakfast is served.

The house stands in peaceful, lawned gardens with a small trout stream flowing through.

As well as peace and quiet, we offer a warm welcome and an easy-going atmosphere.

• Children over 8 only.
• Pets welcome
(not in public rooms)

AA ★★

Fluxton Farm, Ottery St Mary
Devon EX11 1RJ
Tel: 01404 812818 • Fax: 01404 814843
Proprietor Ann Forth • www.fluxtonfarm.co.uk

Paignton

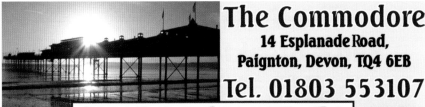

Plymouth, Seaton

SB

Wi-Fi

The Lamplighter
Bed & Breakfast • Plymouth

Situated on the famous Plymouth Hoe, within a short distance of the seafront and historic Barbican, the Lamplighter Guest House is convenient for the city centre, with comprehensive shopping facilities, restaurants and entertainment venues. The naval base H.M.S. Raleigh, is a mere 3 miles on a bus route.

The 9 bedrooms are of the highest standard, all en suite or with private facilities.

- •Tea/coffee/biscuits • Colour TV • Security card entry
- • Full central heating • Full fire certificate
- • Full English Breakfast • Early Breakfast if required
- • Security lit car park • Separate lounge
- • Pets by prior arrangement • Broadband access
- • Special reductions for children sharing with parents

AA
★★★
Guest Accommodation

103 Citadel Road, The Hoe, Plymouth PL1 2RN
Tel: 01752 663855 • stay@lamplighterplymouth.co.uk
www.lamplighterplymouth.co.uk

Beaumont, Castle Hill, Seaton EX12 2QW

Spacious and gracious Victorian, seafront guesthouse in a quiet East Devon town on England's only World Heritage coastline. Shopping, restaurants and leisure facilities nearby. Unrivalled views over Lyme Bay and Beer Cliffs. Half-mile promenade just yards away.
All five rooms en suite with TV, Wi-Fi access, tea and coffee making facilities, radio and hairdryer.
Parking available. Bed and Breakfast from £35 per person per night.
Special weekly rate. A warm welcome is assured.

Gill and Dave Fitzgerald • 01297 20832
e-mail: beaumont.seaton@talktalk.net
www.smoothhound.co.uk/hotels/beaumon1.html

The FHG Directory of Website Addresses
on pages 281-287 is a useful quick reference guide for holiday accommodation with e-mail and/or website details

FREE or **REDUCED RATE** entry to Holiday Visits and Attractions –
see our **READERS' OFFER VOUCHERS** on pages 289-300

SB

SB

Wi-Fi

TOURIST ASSOCIATION

Partridge Arms Farm

Yeo Mill, West Anstey, South Molton, North Devon EX36 3NU

Now a working farm of over 200 acres, four miles west of Dulverton, "Partridge Arms Farm" was once a coaching inn and has been in the same family since 1906. Genuine hospitality and traditional farmhouse fare awaits you. Comfortable accommodation in double, twin and single rooms, which have en suite facilities. There is also an original four-poster bedroom.

Children welcome • Animals by arrangement • Residential licence • Open all year Fishing and riding available nearby • No charge for pets • Group Bookings taken • FARM HOLIDAY GUIDE DIPLOMA WINNER.

www.partridgearmsfarm.co.uk

Bed and Breakfast from £30 Evening Meal £16.

SB

Hazel Milton • Tel: 01398 341217 • Fax: 01398 341569 • e-mail:enquiries@partridgearmsfarm.co.uk

---

The Mill

SB

A warm welcome awaits you at our converted mill, beautifully situated on the banks of the picturesque River Exe. Close to the National Trust's Knightshayes Court and on the route of the Exe Valley Way. Easy access to both the north and south coasts, Exmoor and Dartmoor. Only two miles from Tiverton.

• Relaxing and friendly atmosphere with delicious farmhouse fare.
• En suite bedrooms with TV and tea/coffee making facilities.
• *Bed and Breakfast from £28.*

**Mrs L. Arnold, The Mill, Lower Washfield, Tiverton EX16 9PD
Tel: 01884 255297
e-mail: themillwashfield@hotmail.co.uk
www.themill-tiverton.co.uk**

Please note...

All the information in this book is given in good faith in the belief that it is correct. However, the publishers cannot guarantee the facts given in these pages, neither are they responsible for changes in policy, ownership or terms that may take place after the date of going to press. Readers should always satisfy themselves that the facilities they require are available and that the terms, if quoted, still apply.

Torquay

The Redhouse Hotel & Maxton Lodge

SB

Wi-Fi

We've joined together the friendly service and facilities of the 2 star Redhouse Hotel for those wanting a traditional hotel atmosphere, with the privacy and freedom of Maxton Lodge's 24 self-contained holiday apartments. Two styles of accommodation sharing the same conveniently located grounds and superb range of facilities, so whether you're a working conference delegate or a fun loving family you'll find a style to suit you.

★ Indoor and Outdoor Swimming Pools
★ Spa Pool ★ Gym ★ Sauna
★ Beauty Salon ★ Solarium
★ Launderette ★ Licensed Restaurant
★ Indoor Recreation Room

Redhouse Hotel, Rousdown Road, Chelston, Torquay TQ2 6PB
Tel: (01803) 607811 • Fax: (0871) 5289455
e-mail: stay@redhouse-hotel.co.uk
www.redhouse-hotel.co.uk

The best of both worlds!...

Callisham Farm B&B

Rustic charm in rural Devon countryside

Esme Wills and her family extend a warm welcome to their guests all year round. Feel at home in one of the three comfortable en suite bedrooms, with tea/coffee tray, clock radio and TV. Relax in the warm and cosy guests' lounge.
A superb English breakfast is the perfect beginning to the day; vegetarian and special diets catered for on request.
With easy access to rolling moorland, Callisham is a perfect base for riding, fishing, golf, and touring the beautiful coasts of Devon and Cornwall. In the nearby village of Meavy, the Royal Oak offers a selection of real ales and fine food; other pubs within a mile and a half; Plymouth 12 miles.

www.callisham.co.uk • esme@callisham.co.uk
Meavy, Near Yelverton PL20 6PS • Tel/Fax: 01822 853901

Dorset

In Dorset on the south coast, there are resorts to suit everyone, from traditional, busy Bournemouth with 10 kilometres of sandy beach and a wide choice of entertainment, shopping and dining, to the quieter seaside towns of Seatown, Mudeford and Barton-on-Sea, and Charmouth with its shingle beach. Lulworth Cove is one of several picturesque little harbours. Fossil hunters of all age groups are attracted by the spectacular cliffs of the Jurassic Coast, a World Heritage Site, and walkers can enjoy the wonderful views from the South West Coast Path at the top. With almost half the county included in Areas of Outstanding Natural Beauty, walking enthusiasts have downs, heathland, woodlands and river valleys, country villages and market towns to explore, even into the New Forest, with all it has to offer.

Bournemouth

Denewood is a smart, friendly family hotel, ideally situated to take advantage of the Bournemouth beaches and the new surf reef which are only 500 yards away, the popular Boscombe shopping centre and the famous Opera House. The hotel has a Health and Beauty salon offering a wide range of pampering treatments. For the business traveller there is a complete set of office facilities, plus internet access points.

B&B from £22.50-£42.
Special weekly rates available
and Short Break discounts

All 12 of our bedrooms, which are divided over 2 floors, are individually decorated and have a range of amenities such as a desk and chair, en suite facilities, tea and coffee making equipment and a television.

DENEWOOD HOTEL
40 Sea Road, Bournemouth BH5 1BQ
Tel: 01202 394493 • Fax: 01202 391155
www.denewood.co.uk

SB
Wi-Fi

Alum Dene Hotel

2 Burnaby Road,
Alum Chine,
Bournemouth BH4 8JF
• Tel: 01202 764011 •

Renowned for good old fashioned hospitality and friendly service. Come and be spoilt at our licensed hotel. All rooms en suite, with colour TV. Some have sea views. Only 200 metres from Alum Chine's sandy beach. Car Parking. Christmas House party. No charge for pets. Open all year.

e-mail: alumdenehotel@hotmail.co.uk • www.alumdenehotel.com

Bournemouth B&B
Southernhay Hotel

42 Alum Chine Rd, Westbourne,
Bournemouth BH4 8DX
Tel & Fax: 01202 761251

The Southernhay Hotel provides warm, friendly, high standard accommodation with a large car park and a hearty breakfast. All rooms have central heating, colour TV with Freeview, tea/coffee making facilities and hairdryer. Six bedrooms, four en suite.

The hotel is ideally situated in Westbourne, within walking distance of many bars, restaurants and designer shops. Across the road a path leads through Alum Chine wood, down to miles of safe sandy beaches. The Bournemouth International Centre, cinemas, theatres, restaurants, clubs and pubs are all within easy reach; minutes by car or the frequent bus service. Open all year.

Details from Tom and Lynn Derby. 2 for 1 Golf deals available
Bed and Breakfast from £20 to £30 per adult per night.
Contact Tom or Lynn for last minute offers.

enquiries@southernhayhotel.co.uk • www.southernhayhotel.co.uk

Friendly, family-run hotel with beautiful garden and ample parking. Close to beach and shops. Ideal for exploring Bournemouth, Christchurch and the New Forest. Excellent full English or continental breakfast. Ten en suite rooms, four-poster suite, ground floor rooms (one suitable for a wheelchair) and large family bedrooms. Senior Citizen and child discounts. Dogs welcome free. No smoking.
B&B from £24pppn, from £147pp per week.

SOUTHBOURNE GROVE HOTEL, 96 Southbourne Road,
Southbourne, Bournemouth BH6 3QQ
Tel: 01202 420503 • Fax: 01202 421953
neil@pack1462.freeserve.co.uk
www.southbournegrovehotel.co.uk

Bridport

SB

Wi-Fi

17th Century
FROGMORE FARM

Frogmore is a 90-acre grazing farm situated tranquilly in beautiful West Dorset, overlooking the Jurassic Coast of Lyme Bay, and away from the crowds. Ideal for walking or touring by car, our land is adjacent to National Trust land, to the cliffs and coast (Seatown 1½ miles), and the South West Coastal Path.

One twin and two double bedrooms, all en suite, with TV and tea-making facilities. Guests' dining room and cosy lounge with woodburner. Not suitable for very young children or the infirm due to very steep internal stairs and external steps.

Well behaved dogs very welcome • Open all year

• Car essential • Brochure and terms free on request

• Self-catering also available.

Contact Mrs Sue Norman • Tel: 01308 456159
Frogmore Farm, Chideock, Bridport DT6 6HT • www.frogmorefarm.com
e-mail: bookings@frogmorefarm.com

Wisteria Cottage
Morcombelake, West Dorset

SB

Wi-Fi

Stunning panoramic views from our comfortable, well equipped en suite guest rooms.
A friendly welcome and good food. Vegetarian and special diets also catered for. VisitBritain Breakfast Award.
An ideal base for exploring the Jurassic World Heritage Coast and historic towns of Lyme Regis and Bridport.
A walkers' paradise or just an idyllic spot for people seeking tranquillity and fresh country air. Fossil hunting equipment available for our guests' use.
Off road parking. Visit Britain Four Star Silver Award.
Open all year except Christmas and New Year.
Rooms from £65 - £75 per night for two persons sharing, £45 – £55 single occupancy. Low season midweek breaks also available. Call now for a brochure, or visit our website.

Contact Details:
Taylors Lane, Morcombelake, Dorset DT6 6ED
Tel: 01297 489019
www.dorsetcottage.org.uk
E-mail: dave@dorsetcottage.org.uk

New House Farm

Bed & Breakfast

Situated in beautiful countryside, set in the rural Dorset hills, comfortable farmhouse with large garden where you are welcome to sit or stroll around. Two large rooms available, both en suite, with lovely views. Each room has television, fridge and tea/coffee making facilities. Discover the charm of Bridport, the Chesil Beach and the World Heritage Coastline. Seaside, golf courses, fossil hunting, gardens, wonderful walking, lots to see and do – including our own Coarse Fishing Lake, well stocked with carp, roach and tench. Tickets available from New House Farm.

SB

Wi-Fi

Bed and Breakfast from £30pppn

Jane Greening, New House Farm, Mangerton Lane, Bradpole, Bridport DT6 3SF
Tel & Fax: 01308 422884 • e-mail: mangertonlake@btconnect.com
www.mangertonlake.co.uk

Situated ten minutes' walk from the market town of Bridport, two miles from the Jurassic Coast, ten miles from Lyme Regis and ten miles from the sub-tropical gardens at Abbotsbury, near Weymouth.
Bedrooms with TV, tea making facilities and washbasin. Parking space available.

Mrs K.E. Parsons

179 St Andrews Road, Bridport • 01308 422038

Rosebank   Bed & Breakfast

SB

Rosebank is an attractive period stone cottage located in the peaceful and picturesque village of Corscombe where it nestles in beautiful rolling countryside. Only 30 minutes from the Jurassic Coast. Luxurious king-size four-poster/family room and double room, both with own private bathroom and beautifully refurbished to a very high standard.

Wi-Fi

Rosebank, High Street, Corscombe,
Dorchester, Dorset DT2 0NZ
Telephone - 01935 891936 • Mobile - 07940 927 037
email enquiries: caroline.osmond@btinternet.com
www.rosebank-cottage.co.uk

Dorchester

www.bandbdorchester.co.uk

Nicola and Gary Cutler would like to welcome you to their family run B&B within a few minutes' walk of the historic town of Dorchester.

Wi-Fi

They offer high quality accommodation in relaxed and luxurious surroundings. Bay Tree House is a late 19thC house that has been stylishly and imaginatively refurbished to a high standard. The rooms are spacious and light, and all rooms offer either en suite or private facilities. Double and twin bedded rooms are available; single occupancy subject to availability.

AA

★★★★
Bed & Breakfast

A five minute stroll along tree-lined pavements and avenues will take you straight to the heart of Dorchester's shopping centre, and a five minute stroll in the other direction will take you to Thomas Hardy's town house.

Athelstan Road, Dorchester DT1 1NR

Tel: 01305 263696

e-mail: info@baytreedorchester.com

Nethercroft

This country house with its friendly and homely atmosphere welcomes you to the heart of Hardy's Wessex. Central for touring the many places of interest that Dorset has to offer, including Corfe Castle, Lyme Regis, Dorchester, Weymouth, Lulworth Cove, etc. Lovely country walks and many local attractions.

SB

Two double rooms, one single, en suite or separate bathroom. TV lounge, dining room. Large garden.

Open all year • Central heating • Car essential, ample parking • *B&B from £30.*

Take A35 from Dorchester, we are the last house at the western edge of the village.

Mrs V.A. Bradbeer, Nethercroft, Winterbourne Abbas, Dorchester DT2 9LU

Tel: 01305 889337 • e-mail: val.bradbeer@btconnect.com • www.nethercroft.com

---

Visit the FHG website
www.holidayguides.com
for all kinds of holiday
accommodation in Britain

Pennhills Farmhouse, set in 100 acres of unspoiled countryside, is situated one mile from the village of Shillingstone in the heart of the Blackmore Vale, an ideal peaceful retreat, short break or holiday. It offers spacious comfortable accommodation for all ages; children welcome. One downstairs bedroom. All bedrooms en suite with TV and tea/coffee making facilities, complemented by traditional English breakfast with home produced bacon and sausages. Vegetarians catered for. Good meals available locally. Brochure sent on request. A warm and friendly welcome is assured from your host Rosie Watts. From £30 per person.

AA
★★★
Farmhouse

Pennhills Farm

Mrs Rosie Watts, Pennhills Farm, Sandy Lane, Off Lanchards Lane, Shillingstone, Blandford DT11 0TF
Tel: 01258 860491

Sandhaven Guest House

SB

Wi-Fi

You can be sure of a warm welcome with good home-cooking whenever you stay at Sandhaven. We wish to make sure your stay is as relaxing and enjoyable as possible. All bedrooms are en suite and equipped with tea and coffee making facilities; all have colour TV. There is a residents' lounge, dining room and conservatory for your comfort. The Purbeck Hills are visible from the guest house, as is the beach, which is only 100 metres away.

- *Bed and Breakfast is available from £37.50 to £42.50.*
- *Non-smoking bedrooms.*
- *Open all year except Christmas.*

Janet Foran • Sandhaven Guest House
5 Ulwell Road, Swanage BH19 1LE
Tel: 01929 422322

e-mail: mail@sandhaven-guest-house.co.uk
www.sandhaven-guest-house.co.uk

The White Swan

The Square, 31 High Street, Swanage, Dorset BH19 2LT

THE WHITE
SWAN

SB

Wi-Fi

- Two minutes from the beach
- Traditional pub food • Sunday roasts
- Large beer garden
- En suite accommodation with parking
- Wi-Fi access • TV and pool table
- Best Beer Guide Pub • CAMRA selected.

e-mail: info@whiteswanswanage.co.uk
www.whiteswanswanage.co.uk • 01929 423804

Wareham (near Lulworth)

Gloucestershire

SB

Detmore House
01242 582868

Situated in an area of outstanding natural beauty, Detmore House is a period property set in extensive grounds. It offers spacious en suite rooms with TV, DVD, Wi-Fi and beautiful views. Close to Cheltenham and Gloucester, with restaurants, shops, racecourse and theatres, and a short walk from the Cotswold Way.

London Road, Charlton Kings,
Cheltenham GL52 6UT
gillkilminster@btconnect.com
www.detmorehouse.com

ETC ★★★★

Honeybourne Lane, Mickleton,
Chipping Campden,
Gloucestershire GL55 6PU

Tel: 01386 438890
Fax: 01386 438113
enquiries@brymbo.com
www.brymbo.com

A warm and welcoming farm building conversion with large garden in beautiful Cotswold countryside, ideal for walking and touring.

All rooms are on the ground floor, with full central heating. The comfortable bedrooms all have colour TV and tea/coffee making facilities. Sitting room with open log fire. Breakfast room. Children and dogs welcome. Two double, two twin, one family. Bathrooms: three en suite, two private or shared. Parking. Brochure available. Credit Cards accepted.

Bed and Breakfast: single £35 to £50; double £55 to £75; family from £85.

Close to Stratford-upon-Avon, Broadway, Chipping Campden and with easy access to Oxford and Cheltenham.

SB

Wi-Fi

A warm and friendly welcome awaits you at our completely refurbished 15th century Grade ll Listed farmhouse, in the heart of this beautiful village.

Spacious beamed rooms, inglenook fireplace in the dining room where a full English breakfast is served. Large private car park at rear. All bedrooms are en suite, with coffee/tea making facilities, TV, radio and hairdryer.

Accommodation comprises two double, two twin and one family suite consisting of a single and a double room en suite.

Sorry no pets allowed in the house • Non-smoking • No children under 12.

Terms per night: from £65 per suite, 2 persons sharing. More than two nights from £60. Family room for 3 persons sharing £90.

Veronica Stanley,

Home Farm House,
Ebrington, Chipping Campden
GL55 6NL
Tel & Fax: 01386 593309
willstanley@farmersweekly.net
www.homefarminthecotswolds.co.uk

QUALITY ALL GROUND FLOOR ACCOMMODATION.
"Kilmorie" is Grade II Listed (c1848) within conservation area in a lovely part of Gloucestershire. Only three miles from Hartpury College and 10 miles from Malvern's Three Counties Showground. Gloucester and Tewkesbury seven miles.

Tel: 01452 840224

En suite double, twin, family or single bedrooms, all having tea tray, colour digital TV, radio.
Very comfortable guests' lounge, traditional home cooking is served in the separate diningroom overlooking large garden. Perhaps walk waymarked farmland footpaths which start here.
We have ponies and "free range" hens. Rural yet perfectly situated to visit Cotswolds, Royal Forest of Dean, Wye Valley and Malvern Hills.
Children over four years welcome. Ample parking. Cycle storage. B&B from £30pp.

S.J. Barnfield, "Kilmorie Smallholding"
Gloucester Road, Corse, Staunton, Gloucester GL19 3RQ
e-mail: sheila-barnfield@supanet.com • mobile: 07966 532337

Parkend, Stow-on-the-Wold

THE FOUNTAIN INN & LODGE

Parkend, Royal Forest of Dean, Gloucestershire GL15 4JD

Tel: 01594 562189

Traditional village inn, well known locally for its excellent meals and real ales.

A Forest Fayre menu offers such delicious main courses as Lamb Shank In Redcurrant and Rosemary Sauce, and locally made sausages, together with a large selection of curries, vegetarian dishes, and other daily specials.

Centrally situated in one of England's foremost wooded areas, the inn makes an ideal base for sightseeing, or for exploring some of the many peaceful forest walks nearby.

All bedrooms (including two specially adapted for the less able) are en suite, decorated and furnished to an excellent standard, and have television and tea/coffee making facilities.

e-mail: welcome@thefountaininnandlodge.co.uk
www.thefountaininnandlodge.co.uk

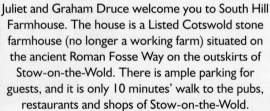

South Hill Farmhouse

Juliet and Graham Druce welcome you to South Hill Farmhouse. The house is a Listed Cotswold stone farmhouse (no longer a working farm) situated on the ancient Roman Fosse Way on the outskirts of Stow-on-the-Wold. There is ample parking for guests, and it is only 10 minutes' walk to the pubs, restaurants and shops of Stow-on-the-Wold.

Single £60, double/twin £75, family (three) £135, (four) £140 per room per night, including generous breakfast. Non-smoking house.

South Hill Farmhouse, Fosseway, Stow-on-the-Wold GL54 1JU
Tel: 01451 831888 • Fax: 01451 832255
e-mail: info@southhill.co.uk
www.southhill.co.uk

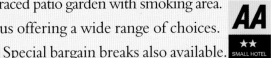

Somerset

Bath

SB

Wi-Fi

Eden Vale Farm

Eden Vale Farm nestles down in a valley by the River Frome. Enjoying a picturesque location, this old watermill offers a selection of rooms including en suite facilities, complemented by an excellent choice of full English or Continental breakfasts. Beckington is an ideal centre for visiting Bath, Longleat, Salisbury, Cheddar, Stourhead and many National Trust Houses including Lacock Village.

Only a ten minute walk to the village pub, three-quarters of a mile of river fishing. Local golf courses and lovely walks.

Very friendly animals. Dogs welcome.

Open all year.

Mrs Barbara Keevil, Eden Vale Farm, Mill Lane, Beckington, Near Frome BA11 6SN • Tel: 01373 830371
e-mail: bandb@edenvalefarm.co.uk • www.edenvalefarm.co.uk

Wi-Fi

The Old Red House

Welcome to our romantic Victorian "Gingerbread" house which is colourful, comfortable and warm; full of unexpected touches and intriguing little curiosities. The leaded and stained glass windows are now double glazed to ensure a peaceful night's stay. All have colour TV with Freeview, complimentary beverages, radio alarm clock, hairdryer and en suite shower.

Easy access to city centre, via road or river paths. The English breakfast and buffet will keep you going all day. We have private parking. Non-smoking.

Theresa Elly, The Old Red House,
37 Newbridge Road, Bath BA1 3HE
01225 330464
e-mail: theoldredhousebath@onebillinternet.co.uk
www.theoldredhousebath.co.uk

Bath

Somerset shares in the wild, heather-covered moorland of Exmoor, along with the Quantock Hills to the east, ideal for walking, mountain biking, horse riding, fishing and wildlife holidays. The forty miles of coastline with cliffs, sheltered bays and sandy beaches includes family resorts like Weston-super-Mare, with its famous donkey rides and brand new pier with 21st century facilities and entertainment for everyone. More family fun can be found at Minehead and Burnham-on-Sea, or opt for the quiet charm of Clevedon. With theatres, festivals, museums, galleries, gardens, sporting events and of course, shopping, the city of Bath has everything for a short break or longer stay. Attracting visitors from all over the world, this designated World Heritage Site boasts wonderful examples of Georgian architecture and of course, the Roman Baths.

Leigh Farm

Bed & Breakfast and Self-Catering Accommodation

Leigh Farm is a working beef and sheep farm, situated at Pensford and close to Bath and Bristol. Bristol International Airport 10 miles approx.

Bed and Breakfast is offered in this 200 year-old comfy, warm farmhouse, with open log fire in the comfortable guest lounge in winter months. Central heating, TV. Accommodation comprises double en suite and family room with private bathroom. Access at all times.

Self Catering Accommodation available in four family bungalows and one bungalow suitable for couples. The open-plan bungalows are very sturdily constructed, with either one or two bedrooms, sleeping 2-4 persons. Regret no smoking, no pets.

**For brochure contact: Josephine Smart,
Leigh Farm, Pensford, Near Bristol BS39 4BA
Tel & Fax: 01761 490281 • www.leighfarmholidays.co.uk**

Brinsea Green Farm

Brinsea Green is a period farmhouse surrounded by open countryside. Set in 500 acres of farmland, it has easy access from the M5, (J21), A38 and Bristol Airport. Close to the Mendip Hills, the historic cities of Bath, Bristol and Wells, plus the wonders of Cheddar Gorge and Wookey Hole.

Wi-Fi

Comfortably furnished en suite/shower bedrooms offer lovely views, complimentary beverage tray, TV, hair dryer and Wi-Fi. Both lounge and dining room have inglenook fireplaces, log fires in winter.

SINGLE FROM £38.00   DOUBLE FROM £62.00

**Mrs Delia Edwards, Brinsea Green Farm
Brinsea Lane, Congresbury, Near Bristol BS49 5JN
Tel: Churchill (01934) 852278**
e-mail: delia@brinseagreenfarm.co.uk
www.brinseagreenfarm.co.uk

Minehead, Porlock, Quantock Hills

Whitecroft Farm B&B

SB

Wi-Fi

A friendly and informal welcome awaits at our recently refurbished family home, set in approximately four acres of beautiful Somerset countryside

We are a short drive from the Market town of Shepton Mallet and the City of Wells. A trip across the stunning Mendip Hills will take you to Bristol airport in about forty minutes. Or you can enjoy our beautiful scenery by choosing from a number of local walks

We offer single, twin or family en suite accommodation and a comfortable guest lounge. Delicious breakfasts feature eggs from our own hens and home-made jams and chutney.

Ample off road parking and outdoor storage is also available.

Single from £40, Twin from £70, Family Room from £85.

Pylle, Shepton Mallet, Somerset BA4 6ST
01749 838692 • whitecroftfarm@btinternet.com
www.whitecroft-bandb.co.uk

THATCHED COUNTRY COTTAGE & GARDEN B&B

SB

Wi-Fi

An old thatched country cottage halfway between Taunton and Honiton, set in the idyllic Blackdown Hills, a designated Area of Outstanding Natural Beauty. Picturesque countryside with plenty of flowers and wildlife. Central for north/south coasts of Somerset, Dorset and Devon. Double/single and family suite with own facilities, TV, tea/coffee.

Large Conservatory/Garden Room and a separate summer house available for guests' relaxation and al fresco meals if preferred.

Evening Meals also available.
Children and small
well behaved dogs welcome.
Open all year.
B&B from £24pppn.

Mrs Pam Parry, Pear Tree Cottage,
Stapley, Churchstanton, Taunton TA3 7QA
Tel: 01823 601224
e-mail: colvin.parry@virgin.net

www.SmoothHound.co.uk/hotels/thatch.html OR www.best-hotel.com/peartreecottage

Taunton

The Old Mill

Grade II Listed former Corn Mill, situated on the edge of a conservation village just two miles from Taunton.

We have two lovely double bedrooms, The Mill Room with en suite facilities overlooking the weir pool, and The Cottage Suite with its own private bathroom, again with views over the river. Both rooms are centrally heated, with TV, generous beverage tray and thoughtful extras. Guests have their own lounge and dining area overlooking the river, where breakfast may be taken from our extensive breakfast menu amidst machinery of a bygone era. We are a non-smoking establishment.

Double from £32.50 – £35pppn
Single occupancy from £50 - £55

Bishop's Hull, Taunton TA1 5AB
Tel: 01823 289732 / 07967 673916
www.theoldmillbandb.co.uk
www.bandbtaunton.co.uk

LOWER MARSH FARM

Wi-Fi

LOWER MARSH FARM
Kingston Road, Taunton TA2 8AB
Tel & Fax: 01823 451331
e-mail: b&b@lowermarshfarm.co.uk
www.lowermarshfarm.co.uk

Jill & Richard look forward to welcoming you to the relaxed, friendly atmosphere of their farmhouse situated at the foot of the Quantock Hills, a peaceful Area of Outstanding Natural Beauty. Located on the northern fringe of Taunton, Lower Marsh Farm is about a mile from the train station and the County Cricket Ground, and within easy reach of the town centre.

There are three well appointed bedrooms: Honeysuckle, a twin-bedded room with own private bathroom; Jasmin, a double room with shower en suite; and the Blue Room, a double-bedded family room with bath en suite. All the rooms have colour TV and tea/coffee making facilities. Free Wi-Fi access.

A traditional full English breakfast is served in the tastefully furnished dining room; guests' lounge with TV. Sorry, no pets.

AA
★★★★
Farmhouse

Bed & Full English Breakfast
Double: from £70.00 per room • Single: from £38.00
Children: (12 Years & under) £12.00 per child per night

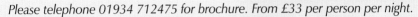

Weston-Super-Mare

MOORLANDS
**Hutton, Near Weston-super-Mare,
Somerset BS24 9QH**

Tel: 01934 812283 • Mobile: 07828 833894

★★★
GUEST HOUSE

Enjoy a good breakfast and warm hospitality at this impressive late Georgian house set in landscaped gardens below the steep wooded slopes of the Western Mendips. A wonderful touring centre, perfectly placed for visits to beaches, sites of special interest and historic buildings. Families with children particularly welcome; reduced terms. Full central heating, open fire in comfortable lounge. Open all year.

Resident host: Mrs Margaret Holt

*Rates: single room from £27-£38
double room from £54-£66 per night.*

e-mail: margaret-holt@hotmail.co.uk

www.moorlandscountryguesthouse.co.uk

Wiltshire

Corsham

SB

Wi-Fi

London (Central & Greater)

The Athena

110-114 SUSSEX GARDENS, HYDE PARK, LONDON W2 1UA
Tel: 0207 706 3866; Fax: 0207 262 6143
e-mail: stay@athenahotellondon.co.uk • www.athenahotel.co.uk

TREAT YOURSELVES TO A QUALITY HOTEL AT AFFORDABLE PRICES

The Athena is a newly completed family run hotel in a restored Victorian building. Professionally designed, including a lift to all floors and exquisitely decorated, we offer our clientele the ambience and warm hospitality necessary for a relaxing and enjoyable stay. Ideally located in a beautiful tree-lined avenue, extremely well-positioned for sightseeing London's famous sights and shops; Hyde Park, Madame Tussaud's, Oxford Street, Marble Arch, Knightsbridge, Buckingham Palace and many more are all within walking distance.

Travel connections to all over London are excellent, with Paddington and Lancaster Gate Stations, Heathrow Express, A2 Airbus and buses minutes away.
Our tastefully decorated bedrooms have en suite bath/shower rooms, satellite colour TV, bedside telephones, tea/coffee making facilities. Hairdryers, trouser press, laundry and ironing facilities available on request. Car parking available.

We offer quality and convenience at affordable rates.

A VERY WARM WELCOME AWAITS YOU.

Single Rooms from £50-£89
Double/Twin Rooms from £64-£99
Triple & Family Rooms from £25 per person
All prices include full English breakfast plus VAT.

All major credit cards accepted, but some charges may apply.

London

Berkshire

Windsor

🪀

SB

🍷

Wi-Fi

Aylesbury

Buckinghamshire

www.country-accom.co.uk/poletrees-farm

Poletrees Farm

This working family farm provides spacious, comfortable 4 Star Bed & Breakfast ground floor accommodation for couples and individuals, whether on an overnight visit or longer.

• Non-smoking

• En suite bedrooms in 4 cottages with colour TV and tea/coffee tray

The Burnwode Jubilee Way cuts through the farm, and there are many places of historic interest in the area.

Ludgershall Road, Brill, Near Aylesbury, Bucks HP18 9TZ • Tel & Fax: 01844 238276

For deposits and bookings please phone or fax
e-mail: poletrees.farm@btinternet.com

AA ★★★★ Guest Accommodation

symbols 🐕🐎SB♿️♉Wi-Fi

🐕	Pets Welcome	🐎	Children Welcome
SB	Short Breaks	♿️	Suitable for Disabled Guests
♉	Licensed	Wi-Fi	Wi-Fi available

Barton-on-Sea

Hampshire

Ideally situated for the delights of the New Forest, scenic cliff top walks, local beaches, pleasure cruises to the Isle of Wight, the Needles and historic Hurst Castle, horse riding, cycling, golf and a whole host of indoor and outdoor pursuits. Laurel Lodge is a comfortable, centrally heated, converted bungalow, offering twin, double and family rooms. All rooms are fully en suite with tea and coffee making facilities, comfortable chairs, colour TV and alarm clock radio. Ground floor rooms available. Breakfast is served in our conservatory/diningroom with views over the garden.

Lee & Melanie Snook, Laurel Lodge,
48 Western Avenue, Barton-on-Sea, New Milton BH25 7PZ
Tel: 01425 618309

Laurel Lodge

Bed and Breakfast from £30.00pp
Special deals for longer breaks
Children welcome, cot supplied by prior arrangement
Off-road parking for all rooms
Strictly no smoking
Open all year
Please phone for further details.

Idyllic countryside, sandy beaches, beautiful gardens and historic houses, country parks, museums and castles, and wildlife parks, are all there to enjoy in Hampshire. There are museums full of military heritage on land, sea and air, including the HMS Victory at Portsmouth, where a trip to the top of the Spinnaker Tower provides spectacular views of the surrounding area. Outdoors walk, cycle or ride on horseback over the heathland and through the ancient woodlands of the New Forest, and in the South Downs National Park, or try out one of the many watersports available along the coast. Boating enthusiasts will make for one of the many marinas, and the annual regatta on the River Hamble, and for courses on sailing, rockclimbing, and even skiing, where better to learn more than the Calshot Activities Centre on the shores of the Solent.

Hook, Lymington

SB
Wi-Fi

OAKLEA GUEST HOUSE

**London Road,
Hook RG27 9LA
Tel: 01256 762673**
Please quote FHG

Friendly, family-run Guest House. All bedrooms en suite with TV and hospitality tray. Ample parking. Easy access from J5 M3, London 55 minutes by train.

Free wireless internet access available via own equipment.

GOLF: Many excellent courses within 10-mile radius.
HORSE RACING at Sandown, Ascot and Goodwood.
SHOPPING at The Oracle, Reading and Festival Place, Basingstoke.
DAYS OUT: Thorpe Park, Chessington, Legoland, Windsor Castle, Hampton Court, RHS Wisley, Milestones.

AA
★★★★
Guest House

e-mail: reception@oakleaguesthouse.co.uk • www.oakleaguesthouse.co.uk

Set in its own grounds in a quiet location, this delightful 1912 period house offers a friendly and relaxed atmosphere, a high standard of accommodation and ample parking.

A delicious choice of breakfasts is served in the spacious residents' dining room.

Only five minutes' walk from the High Street and Quay area, ideal for mariners and for travellers catching Isle of Wight ferries.

Delightful forest and coastal walks.
Open all year.

The Rowans, 76 Southampton Road, Lymington SO41 3GZ
Tel: 01590 672276 • www.rowanshouse.co.uk

The FHG Directory of Website Addresses

on pages 281-287 is a useful quick reference guide for holiday accommodation with e-mail and/or website details

FREE or **REDUCED RATE** entry to Holiday Visits and Attractions –
see our **READERS' OFFER VOUCHERS** on pages 289-300

Efford Cottage

Everton, Lymington,
Hampshire SO41 0JD

Tel: 01590 642315

SB

Wi-Fi

Guests receive a warm and friendly welcome to our home, which is a spacious Georgian cottage. All rooms are en suite with many extra luxury facilities. We offer a four-course, multi-choice breakfast with homemade bread and preserves. Patricia is a qualified chef and uses our home-grown produce. An excellent centre for exploring both the New Forest and the South Coast, with sports facilities, fishing, bird watching and horse riding in the near vicinity. Private parking. Dogs welcome. Sorry, no children. Bed and Breakfast from £25–£35 pppn. Mrs Patricia J. Ellis.

Winner of " England For Excellence 2000"
FHG Diploma 1997/1999/2000/2003 / Michelin / Welcome Host
Awards Achieved: Gold Award / RAC Sparkling Diamond & Warm Welcome
Nominated Landlady of Year & Best Breakfast Award.
Enquiries and bookings by telephone only.

AA ★★★★ Guest Accommodation

e-mail: pellis48@btinternet.com • www.effordcottage.co.uk

Bed & Breakfast Guest Accommodation

SB

Wi-Fi

A delightful character house with a warm, friendly atmosphere. Set in a quiet area of the unspoilt village of Milford-on-Sea and just a few minutes' walk to both sea and village, it is ideally situated for visiting the New Forest, Bournemouth, Salisbury and the Isle of Wight. The comfortable bedrooms are all en suite, with TV, DVD, hospitality tray and many extra touches. Award-winning breakfast menu with many choices. Large sunny diningroom and cosy guest lounge. Attractive gardens and summer house. Ample private parking. Non-smoking. Self-catering apartment also available. Open all year.

Carolyn and Roy Plummer, Ha'penny House,
16 Whitby Road, Milford-on-Sea, Lymington SO41 0ND • 01590 641210
info@hapennyhouse.co.uk • www.hapennyhouse.co.uk

£72-£89 per room per night, double or twin, including breakfast.

AA ★★★★★ Guest Accommodation

NEW FOREST. Mrs J. Pearce, "St Ursula", 30 Hobart Road, New Milton BH25 6EG (01425 613515).
Large detached family home offering every comfort in a friendly relaxed atmosphere. Off Old Milton Road, New Milton. Ideal base for visiting New Forest with its ponies and beautiful walks; Salisbury, Bournemouth easily accessible. Sea one mile. Leisure centre with swimming pool etc, town centre and mainline railway to London minutes away. Twin (en suite), double, family, single rooms, all with handbasin, TV and tea-making facilities. High standards maintained throughout; excellent beds. Two bathrooms/showers, four toilets. Cot etc, available. Pretty garden which guests are welcome to use. Two diningrooms. Smoke detectors installed. Full central heating.

Rates: Bed and Breakfast from £30.00.
• Downstairs twin bedroom suitable for disabled persons.• Children and pets welcome.• Open all year.
N.F.T.A. Quality Assessment *NATIONAL ACCESSIBLE SCHEME LEVEL 1.*

SB

Wi-Fi

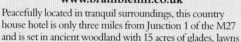

Bramble Hill Hotel

Bramshaw, New Forest, Hampshire SO43 7JG
023 80 813165 • bramblehill@hotmail.co.uk
www.bramblehill.co.uk

Peacefully located in tranquil surroundings, this country house hotel is only three miles from Junction 1 of the M27 and is set in ancient woodland with 15 acres of glades, lawns and shrubbery to enjoy. Ideal for country walks and horse riding.
A short drive from many places of interest including Salisbury, Stonehenge, Winchester and Beaulieu.
All bedrooms have en suite bathrooms and some have antique four-poster beds.
A warm, friendly welcome and a hearty home-cooked breakfast assured.
Daily rates or weekly terms — please phone for details.

SB

Wi-Fi

Twin Oaks
GUEST HOUSE

A warm welcome awaits in Twin Oaks Guest House in Hedge End town. Home-from-home comforts include modern en suite rooms with tea/coffee making facilities and television, and hearty breakfasts. Central heating. Car parking. No smoking.

Close to hotels/function centres, superstores and amenities, including county cricket ground (The Ageas Bowl) and leisure centre. Situated near J7 of the M27 and therefore close to all routes to Portsmouth, Fareham, Winchester and Eastleigh. Also conveniently located close to Swanwick Marina and the Hamble Valley Country Park.

43 Upper Northam Road, Hedge End, Southampton SO30 4EA
Tel: 01489 690054 • Mobile: 07840 816052
e-mail: reservations@twinoaksguesthouse.co.uk
www.twinoaksguesthouse.co.uk

Chale

Isle of Wight

The ultimate sailing destination is of course the Isle of Wight, only a short ferry ride away from the mainland, with marinas, golden, sandy beaches, water sports centres, seakayaking, diving, sailing and windsurfing. On land there are over 500 miles of interconnected footpaths, cycleways, historic castles, dinosaur museums, theme parks and activity centres, or view it all from the skies on a paragliding adventure. To the north and east the well-known resorts of Sandown, Shanklin, Ryde and Ventnor provide all the traditional seaside activities, as well as the sailing centre, Cowes, while West Wight, an Area of Outstanding Natural Beauty will appeal to nature lovers and birdwatchers. With a thriving arts community, and of course two internationally renowned music festivals held every year, there is something for everyone!.

SB

Wi-Fi

Seahorses

A peaceful and beautiful 19th century rectory set in two-and-a-half acres of lovely gardens, just two minutes' drive from Freshwater Bay.
- Good area for walking, golfing, sailing, paragliding and bird watching.
- Close to National Trust areas.

Double, family and twin rooms, all en suite. TV lounge, log fires. Children and pets welcome. *B&B pppn: £33-£39 depending on season. Children half price.*

Brenda & Boris Moscoff, Seahorses, Victoria Road, Freshwater, IOW PO40 9PP
Tel/Fax: 01983 752574
seahorses-iow@tiscali.co.uk
www.seahorsesisleofwight.com

SB

Wi-Fi

The Dorset Hotel is situated close to six miles of sandy beaches, Esplanade, Ryde Shopping Centre & transport routes. Most bedrooms are en suite and all have colour TV and hospitality tray, some have sea view.

Residents' bar, comfortable TV lounge.

Free car park. Breakfast is served in the attractively appointed Dining Room.

From £25.00 per person per night.

Ferry Inclusive Packages can be arranged.

The Dorset Hotel

31 Dover Street, Ryde, Isle of Wight PO33 2BW
Tel: 01983 564327 • Fax: 01983 614635
e-mail: hoteldorset@aol.com
www.thedorsethotel.co.uk

Ashford, Broadstairs

Kent

Canterbury

Kent, the 'Garden of England', yet with such easy access to London, is a county of gentle, rolling downlands, edged by the famous White Cliffs and miles of sands and shingle beaches along the Channel coast. Walk along the North Downs Way through an Area of Outstanding Natural Beauty stretching from Kent through Sussex to Surrey, or enjoy the stunning scenery from the Saxon Shore Way with views to the coast of France, and the wildlife of the Medway Estuary and Romney Marsh. The resorts of the Isle of Thanet and the south-east coast, like Ramsgate, Margate, Herne Bay and Deal have plenty to offer for a traditional family seaside holiday, and there are steam trains, animal parks and castles full of history to explore too. At Leeds and Hever Castles visitors can even play a round of golf, just two of the wide choice of links, urban and countryside courses throughout the county.

Banbury, Bicester

Oxfordshire

NEW FARMHOUSE situated on edge of village off A423 Southam Road, three miles north of Banbury overlooking the beautiful Cherwell Valley. Ideally situated for touring Cotswolds, Stratford, Warwick, Oxford, Blenheim Palace. There are local pubs serving meals. Very comfortable accommodation comprising one twin room, one family room (one double and one single bed). Tea/coffee making facilities, hair dryers; central heating; shower room with electric shower; guests' sittingroom with colour TV. All rooms fully carpeted. Non-smoking. Parking. Food standards Authority Hygiene rating 5 – Very Good *Sorry, no pets.*

Bed and Breakfast from £25
Child under 10 sharing family room £12
A warm welcome awaits you

Mrs Rosemary Cannon
High Acres Farm
Great Bourton
Banbury OX17 1RL
Tel : 01295 750217
e-mail: RCHAF@aol.com

Tower Fields

Tusmore Road, Near Souldern
Bicester OX27 7HY

SB
Wi-Fi

Ground floor en suite rooms, all with own entrance and ample parking. Rooms have power showers, tea/coffee making facilities, fridges, Freeview TV, etc. Breakfast using local produce.

Easy reach of Banbury, Oxford, Stratford-upon-Avon, many National Trust houses. Motor racing at Silverstone, horse racing at Towcester or a leisurely cruise down the Oxford Canal. Shopaholics catered for at nearby Bicester Village retail shopping outlet.

A friendly welcome awaits you - dogs and horses welcome by arrangement.
Children over 10 years only.

Toddy and Clive Hamilton-Gould
01869 346554
toddyclive@towerfields.com
www.towerfields.com

Oxfordshire, with the lively, historic university city of Oxford, the 'city of dreaming spires', at its centre, is ideal for a relaxing break. Quiet countryside is dotted with picturesque villages and busy market towns, while the open downland to the south is covered by a network of footpaths connecting up with the ancient Ridgeway Trail and the riverside walks of the Thames Path. Hire a rowing boat or a punt for a leisurely afternoon on the River Thames or explore the Cotswold villages to the west. Stretching from Oxford to the Cotswolds, the mysterious Vale of the White Horse is named after the oldest chalk figure in Britain, dating back over 3000 years. The historic market towns like Abingdon and Wantage make good shopping destinations, and all the family will enjoy the history, activities and beautiful gardens at Blenheim Palace.

SB

Wi-Fi

symbols 🐎🎠SB&♀Wi-Fi

🐕	Pets Welcome	🎠	Children Welcome
SB	Short Breaks	&	Suitable for Disabled Guests
♀	Licensed	Wi-Fi	Wi-Fi available

Horley

Surrey

Visit the FHG website
www.holidayguides.com
for all kinds of holiday
accommodation in Britain

East Sussex

Paskins
town house

Distin

PASKINS is a small, green hotel that has found its own way. It's an eclectic, environmentally friendly hotel with nice and sometimes amusing rooms, with the bonus of brilliant breakfasts. You arrive at the Art Nouveau reception to be shown to one of the 19 slightly out of the ordinary rooms, each individual in design, perhaps a little quirky, but not at the expense of being comfortable. For example, one room has a genuine Victorian brass bed with several mattresses, just as Queen Victoria's did, which enabled her to sleep higher than all her subjects. Having been welcomed royally, you will sleep like a monarch, and come down to a regal spread at breakfast, prepared with mainly organic, fair trade or locally sourced produce. The Art Deco breakfast room continues the charming theme of the hotel, and has a menu of celebrated choice, including a variety of imaginative vegetarian and vegan dishes, some intriguing signature dishes, and a blackboard full of specials.

Paskins
SCORES
ON THE DOORS

Healthy
Choice
Gold
Award

AA
★★★★
Guest
Accommodation

Green
Tourism
GOLD

AA
Breakfast
Award

PASKINS TOWN HOUSE •18/19 Charlotte Street, Brighton BN2 1AG
Tel: 01273 601203 • Fax: 01273 621973
www.paskins.co.uk • welcome@paskins.co.uk

West Sussex

SB

Wi-Fi

• *Woodacre* •

offers Bed and Breakfast in a traditional family home with accommodation for up to 10-12 guests. The house is set in a large and beautiful garden. We are well positioned for Chichester, Arundel, Goodwood and the seaside and easily accessible from the A27. Our rooms are clean and spacious and two are on the ground floor. We serve a full English breakfast in our conservatory or diningroom overlooking the garden. Plenty of parking space. Everyone is very welcome.

Credit cards accepted.

Mrs Vicki Richards,
Woodacre, Arundel Road,
Fontwell, Arundel BN18 0QP
Tel: 01243 814301
e-mail: wacrebb@aol.com
www.woodacre.co.uk

Bed and Breakfast from £30.00 per person.
3 nights for the price of 2 November to March.

From the dramatic cliffs and sandy beaches of the Sussex coast to the quiet countryside of the Weald and the South Downs, there's an endless choice of the things to do and places to explore. Sailing, walking, cycling, horse riding, golf are all available for an active break, while the fascinating history of 1066 country, castles like Bodiam and the seaside ports will attract all the family. If you're looking for beaches, the 100 miles of coast offer something for everyone, whether your preference is for action-packed fun at a family resort or a quiet, remote spot. Best known for a combination of lively nightlife and all the attractions of the seaside, Brighton has everything from its pebble beach, classic pier, Royal Pavilion and Regency architecture, to shopping malls, art galleries, antique shops, and the specialist boutiques and coffee shops of The Lanes. There's so much to choose from!

Selsey

SB

ST ANDREWS LODGE

Chichester Road, Selsey, West Sussex PO20 0LX
Tel: 01243 606899 • Fax: 01243 607826

Welcome to St Andrews Lodge, the perfect place for a relaxing break. Situated in the small seaside town of Selsey and well located for Chichester and the South Downs; close to unspoilt beaches and 5 minutes from Pagham Harbour Nature Reserve. Enjoy our delicious breakfast and stay in one of our individually decorated rooms. All rooms have hospitality tray and ironing facilities. Fridges in some of the rooms. Some rooms open on to our large garden to allow your dog to stretch his legs. No charge for dogs but donation to local nature reserve welcome. Licensed bar, wheelchair accessible room, large car park.

Please apply for brochure and details of our special winter offer.

info@standrewslodge.co.uk
www.standrewslodge.co.uk

Burwell

Cambridgeshire

THE MEADOW HOUSE
**2a High Street, Burwell,
Cambridge CB25 0HB**
Tel: 01638 741926
Fax: 01638 741861

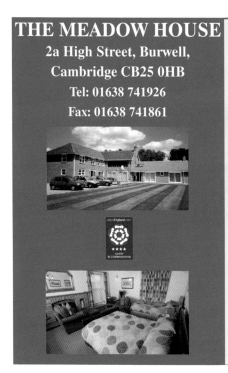

The Meadow House is a magnificent modern house set in two acres of wooded grounds offering superior Bed and Breakfast accommodation in spacious rooms, some with king-size beds. The variety of en suite accommodation endeavours to cater for all requirements; a suite of rooms sleeping six complete with south-facing balcony; a triple room on the ground floor with three single beds and the Coach House, a spacious annexe with one double and one single bed; also one double and two twins sharing a well equipped bathroom. All rooms have TV, central heating and tea/coffee facilities. Car parking. No smoking
Family rate available on request.
e-mail: hilary@themeadowhouse.co.uk
www.themeadowhouse.co.uk
www.hilaryscottage.co.uk

Cambridgeshire immediately brings to mind the ancient university city of Cambridge, lazy hours punting on the river past the imposing college buildings, students on bicycles, museums and bookshops. This cosmopolitan centre has so much to offer, with theatres, concerts varying from classical to jazz, an annual music festival, cinemas, botanic gardens, exciting shops and to round it all off, restaurants, pubs and cafes serving high quality food. In the surrounding countryside historic market towns, pretty villages and stately homes wait to be explored. Visit Ely with its magnificent cathedral and museum exhibiting the national collection of stained glass, antique shops and cafes. Shopping is one of the attractions of Peterborough, along with Bronze Age excavations and reconstructed dwelling, a ghost tour of the museum and an annual CAMRA Beer Festival.

Cambridge

Manor Farm

Landbeach, Cambridge CB25 9FD
Tel: 01223 860165

Wi-Fi

Manor Farm is a lovely Georgian house with large spacious bedrooms, all with en suite or private bathroom, and a light airy sitting room that guests may use. Wifi available. Guests are welcome to relax in the large walled garden or take a walk on the farm.

Landbeach is a small, pretty village about six miles north of Cambridge and ten miles south of Ely. There are many local pubs and restaurants, although none are within walking distance - why not bring a bicycle and cycle along the tow path into Cambridge? There is also a local bus service and a mainline train service from the next village.

Ample off road parking.

Terms from £50 per room single, £60 double and £75 triple.

e-mail: vhatley@btinternet.com • www.manorfarmcambridge.co.uk

- Within walking distance of city centre.
- Single, double/twin and family bedrooms, all en suite.
- All rooms with colour TV, hairdryer, tea/coffee making facilities, iron etc.
- Varied breakfast menu served in dining room overlooking picturesque garden.
- On-site parking; easy access to A14, M11, A10.

57 Arbury Road, Cambridge CB4 2JB
Tel: 01223 350086
www.victoria-guesthouse.co.uk
e-mail: victoriahouse@ntlworld.com

Victoria
Guest House

Kelvedon

Essex

Highfields Farm

Set in a quiet area on a 700-acre working farm. This makes a peaceful overnight stop on the way to Harwich or a base to visit historic Colchester and Constable country. Convenient for Harwich, Felixstowe and Stansted Airport. Easy access to A12 and main line trains to London. The accommodation comprises one twin and two double bedrooms, all en suite, with TV and tea/coffee making facilities. Residents' lounge. Good English breakfast is served in the oak beamed dining room.

Ample parking • No smoking • Bed and Breakfast from £42-£44 single and £62-£64 twin or double.

Mrs D. Bunting, Highfields Farm, Highfields Lane, Kelvedon CO5 9BJ • Tel & Fax: 01376 570334
e-mail: highfieldsfarm@tiscali.co.uk • www.highfieldsfarm.co.uk

Wi-Fi

From the historic port of Harwich in the north to the Thames estuary in the south, the 300 miles of coastline and dry climate of maritime Essex have attracted holiday makers since early Victorian times. Nowadays there's plenty for everyone, from the fun family resorts with plenty of action like Clacton, on the Essex sunshine coast, and Southend-on-Sea, with over six miles of clean safe sand and the world's longest pleasure pier to quiet walks through country nature reserves. Along the coast there are quiet clifftop paths, sheltered coves, long beaches, mudflats, saltmarshes and creeks. Previously the haunt of smugglers, these are now a great attraction for birdwatchers, particularly for viewing winter wildfowl. At Maldon take a trip on a Thames barge to see the seal colonies or cross the Saxon causeway to Mersea Island to taste the oysters, washed down by wine produced on the vineyard there, but watch the tides!

symbols SB Wi-Fi

	Pets Welcome		*Children Welcome*
SB	*Short Breaks*		*Suitable for Disabled Guests*
	Licensed	Wi-Fi	*Wi-Fi available*

Hertfordshire

HIGH HEDGES is a family-run B & B in the village of Green Tye, 20 minutes from Stansted Airport, M11, Junction 8 and 5 minutes from the village of Much Hadham.
Accommodation consists of comfortably furnished double/single rooms (cot available on request), all with en-suite or private bathrooms, coffee/tea making facilities, hair dryer and TV.
Local produce is used wherever possible for breakfast. Long stay parking available by arrangement.
We now offer holistic therapies from a qualified therapist. So you can enhance your stay by relaxing and enjoying a luxury therapy to take your mind off the stresses of daily life.

Green Tye, Much Hadham,
Herts SG10 6JP
Tel: 01279 842505
e-mail: info@high-hedges.co.uk
www.high-hedges.co.uk

AA
★★★★
Bed & Breakfast

Rickmansworth

Norfolk

Along the Norfolk coast from King's Lynn to Great Yarmouth the broad, sandy beaches, grassy dunes, nature reserves, windmills, and pretty little fishing villages are inviting at all times of year. Following the routes of the Norfolk Coastal Path and Norfolk Coast Cycle Way, walk or cycle between the picturesque villages, stopping to visit the interesting shops and galleries, or to enjoy the seafood at a traditional pub or a restaurant. Take lessons in surfing at Wells-next-the-Sea, then enjoy the challenge of the waves at East Runton or Cromer, or go sea fishing here, or at Sheringham or Mundesley. An important trade and fishing port from medieval times, the historic centre of King's Lynn is well worth a visit, and take a break at Great Yarmouth for family entertainment, 15 miles of sandy beaches, traditional piers, a sea life centre and nightlife with clubs and a casino.

Aylsham

THE OLD PUMP HOUSE

Wi-Fi

LUXURY BED & BREAKFAST ACCOMMODATION

This comfortable 1750s house, owned by Marc James and Charles Kirkman, faces the old thatched pump and is a minute from Aylsham's church and historic marketplace.

It offers five en suite bedrooms (including one four-poster and two family rooms) in a relaxed and elegant setting, with colour TV, tea/coffee making facilities, bath robes, hairdryers and CD radio alarm clocks in all rooms.
Wireless internet access in all rooms.

English breakfast with free-range eggs and local produce (or vegetarian breakfast) is served in the pine-shuttered sitting room overlooking the peaceful garden.

Aylsham is central for Norwich, the coast, the Broads, National Trust houses, steam railways and unspoilt countryside.

- Well behaved children welcome. • Non-smoking.
- Off-road parking for six cars.
- *B&B: single £80-£98, double/twin £98-£120, family room £123-£145*

Holman Road, Aylsham, Norwich
NR11 6BY
Tel: 01263 733789
theoldpumphouse@btconnect.com
www.theoldpumphouse.com

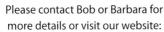

The many RSPB and other nature reserves always attract birdwatchers to the region,
whether for the migrating birds on the coastal sandspits and marshes, or inland on the low-
lying Fens, the Norfolk Broads or the ancient pine forests and heathland of The Breck. Follow
the walking, cycling and horse riding trails, or explore interesting market towns and
villages from the calm waterways of the Broads to see the Norman churches, take part in
the fun of a village fete, watch traditional morris dancing, or visit the one of the few
remaining windmills, at Denver, Letheringsett or Great Bircham. In contrast, in the medieval
city of Norwich with its historic streets and half-timbered houses, cathedral, Norman castle
and museums you'll find not only history, but opera, ballet, theatre, music and restaurants
as well as all kinds of shopping.

THE HARBOUR VIEW

BED & BREAKFAST | RESTAURANT | WEDDINGS | CONFERENCES

The Harbour View is a Victorian Farmhouse with converted barns, combining a taste of the countryside with the modern facilities required by families and business people alike. Set on the banks of the River Nene, we are within easy reach of Sandringham and are situated on the fringes of The Wash, home to some of the most diverse wildlife in the UK.

We offer 11 modern bedrooms - Standard, Executive and Family rooms. The feature rooms are our fabulously decorated four-poster bedrooms, some of which enjoy fantastic views over the stunning Lincolnshire countryside.

There is a small leisure facility on the ground floor, with fitness equipment, pool table and sauna. This is complimentary to all hotel guests. Wi-Fi available in bedrooms and public areas.

We are a family-friendly hotel and welcome children of all ages. Although we do not accept pets in the rooms we can accommodate cats and dogs in our secure kennels.

The Harbour View
East Bank Farm, Garners Lane, Sutton Bridge,
Spalding, Lincolnshire PE12 9YP
Telephone: 01406 351 333 • www.theharbourview.co.uk

Machrimore

Formerly part of an an old manor house, Machrimore is set in attractive gardens with lovely views across to the St Nicholas church tower. The peacefulness and serenity of our location brings our guests back year after year.

Wi-Fi

The accommodation comprises three colour coordinated bedrooms. One double and two twin rooms have en suite facilities, Sky TV, Wi-Fi, clock radio, hair dryer, and tea-coffee making facilities.

We pride ourselves on our Aga-cooked breakfasts. All produce is locally sourced: sausages are from the Norfolk 'Butcher of the Year', we use chestnut mushrooms and free range eggs; locally smoked kippers are available on request.

Guests have their own private garden area and patio accessed directly from the ground floor bedrooms.

Prices from £40 to £42pp daily.
10% discount four nights or more.
Regret, no pets.

Mrs Dorothy MacCallum,
Machrimore, Burnt Street,
Wells-next-the-Sea NR23 1HS
01328 711653
e-mail: enquiries@machrimore.co.uk
www.machrimore.co.uk

Fishermans Return

A hidden gem in the Norfolk countryside

Welcome to the Fishermans Return, a 300 year old brick and flint Freehouse situated in the picturesque unspoilt Norfolk village of Winterton-on-Sea. Long stretches of sandy beaches and beautiful walks are all within a few minutes of the pub.

The Inn is popular with locals and visitors alike, serving excellent food, from simple bar snacks to more substantial fare, with a good choice of local real ales and fine wines. Our food is freshly prepared and we use locally sourced ingredients where we can. Being close to the sea, fish naturally features prominently on our specials board.
Well behaved dogs are most welcome.

Accommodation is available on a B&B basis, in three beautifully appointed and recently renovated rooms, each with comfortable double or twin bed, quality fittings, a flat screen TV & drinks facilities in the room. Full English breakfast is included.

We look forward to welcoming you soon!

For more information and to book, please call us on **01493 393305**
or email: **enquiries@fishermansreturn.com**
www. fishermansreturn.com

Fishermans Return, The Lane, Winterton-on-Sea, Norfolk NR29 4BN

Wroxham Park Lodge

SB

Guest House

Friendly Bed and Breakfast in an elegant
Victorian house in Wroxham, part of the
Norfolk Broads. All rooms en suite, TV, radio, tea/coffee. Famed hearty
breakfasts. Large garden with patio, car park. Ideal for touring Norfolk,
boat trips and hire, walking, cycling, fishing, steam railways, gardens,
zoos and historic houses. Near North Norfolk coast, Norwich and
Great Yarmouth.   *Bed and Breakfast from £48 to £70.*

Wroxham Park Lodge, 142 Norwich Road, Wroxham, Norwich, Norfolk NR12 8SA
Tel: 01603 782991 • e-mail: parklodge@computer-assist.net • www.wroxhamparklodge.com

Home Farm

Comfortable accommodation set in four acres, quiet location, secluded garden. Conveniently situated off A11 between Attleborough and Wymondham, an excellent location for Snetterton and only 20 minutes from Norwich and 45 minutes from the Norfolk Broads.
Accommodation comprises two double rooms and one single-bedded room, all with TV, tea/coffee facilities and central heating. Children over five years old welcome, but sorry no animals and no smoking. Fishing lakes only ½ mile away.

Bed and Breakfast from £30pppn.

Mrs Joy Morter, Home Farm,
Morley, Wymondham NR18 9US
Tel: 01953 602581

Visit the FHG website
www.holidayguides.com
for all kinds of holiday
accommodation in Britain

Suffolk

SB

Wi-Fi

Clare is an historic market town and the area abounds in history and ancient buildings, with many antique shops and places of interest to visit. The house is within easy walking distance of the ancient castle and country park, and the town centre with pubs and restaurants which provide excellent food. Easy parking.
Bed and Breakfast from £48pppn
Pets and children by arrangement.

COBBLES
BED &
BREAKFAST
IN CLARE

Within the pretty walled garden is the charming beamed twin-bedded en suite cottage with its own access. The cottage has central heating, fridge, colour TV and tea/coffee making facilities.

Alastair and Woolfy Tuffill, Cobbles, 26 Nethergate Street, Clare, Near Sudbury CO10 8NP • 01787 277539
e-mail: enquiries@cobblesclare.co.uk
www.cobblesclare.co.uk

HIGH HOUSE FARM

SB

Wi-Fi

Farmhouse Bed & Breakfast

High House Farm is a family-run farm in the heart of rural Suffolk, offering quality Bed & Breakfast in our 15th Century listed farmhouse.

Featuring: exposed oak beams • inglenook fireplaces • generous Full English Breakfast with locally sourced ingredients • tea and coffee making facilities • flat screen TVs • one double room, en suite and one large family room with double and twin beds and private adjacent bathroom
children's cots • high chairs • books • toys • outside play equipment • attractive semi-moated gardens • farm and woodland walks.
Explore the heart of rural Suffolk, local vineyard, Easton Farm Park, Framlingham and Orford Castles, Parham Air Museum, Saxtead Windmill, Minsmere, Snape Maltings, Woodland Trust.

High House Farm
Cransford, Framlingham, Woodbridge IP13 9PD
Tel: 01728 663461
e-mail: b&b@highhousefarm.co.uk • www.highhousefarm.co.uk

SB

Sweffling Hall Farm

Set well back from the main Framlingham-Saxmundham road, in a quiet location with pond and garden. We have chickens providing free-range eggs. Convenient for Woodland Trust (nearby), Framlingham Castle, Saxstead Mill and Coast. Only 9 miles away is Aldeburgh and Minsmere Bird Reserve. Ideal for walking and cycling; vintage transport can be provided free for those staying longer. Two double rooms with private/en suite bathroom and a family room with one double bed and two single beds. There is also a garden with a large pond that can be viewed from the family room.

SWEFFLING HALL FARM
Sweffling, Saxmundham IP17 2BT
Tel & Fax: 01728 663644
e-mail: stephen.mann@hotmail.co.uk
www.swefflinghallfarm.co.uk

A warm welcome awaits you at our exceptional moated farmhouse dating from the 13th Century, and set in extensive grounds including Ace all weather tennis court, in a superb spot two and a half miles north of Dennington, 13 miles from Woodbridge. A comfortable base with log fires in winter and plenty of beams. Close to Snape Maltings, the coast, Minsmere and many places of interest. Accommodation comprises one double and one twin bedroom, or two twins let as singles; guests' own bathroom and sitting room. Good pubs nearby. Bread and marmalade home made.

Parking available • Non-smoking.
B&B from £34 Single, £68 Double/Twin.

GRANGE FARM
Dennington, Woodbridge IP13 8BT
Tel: 01986 798388 • mobile: 07774 182835
www.grangefarm.biz

Derbyshire

Compton House
Guest House in Ashbourne

Compton House is situated in the charming historic market town of Ashborne, with its fine Georgian architecture. We are a family-run guest house with accent on good food and accommodation, and a warm friendly atmosphere.

There are five bedrooms, all en suite, with colour TV, radio, and hairdryer, plus a well stocked tea and coffee tray. All rooms have double beds, and the two larger rooms also have a single bed, so can be used as twin or family rooms. Two rooms can be let as single rooms if required; one of the double rooms is on the ground floor overlooking the garden. Free Wi-Fi.

From peaks to dales to caverns, pretty thatched cottages to majestic stately homes, steam trains to boating lakes, rolling green fields to rocky crags, rivers to streams; whether you want to drive, or ride, walk or climb, cycle or sail, all are on offer in the beautiful Peak District Countryside.

Rooms from £40 to £85 per night

27-31 Compton, Ashbourne DE6 1BX
Tel: 01335 343100
e-mail: jane@comptonhouse.co.uk • www.comptonhouse.co.uk

AA
★★★★
Guest
Accommodation

Causeway House
B&B

SB

Wi-Fi

Back Street, Castleton,
Hope Valley S33 8WE
01433 623291
email: info@causewayhouse.co.uk
www.causewayhouse.co.uk
Causeway House is a 16th Century Cruck Cottage in the heart of Castleton in the beautiful Peak District. The area is renowned for its scenery, history and heritage with amazing walks, cycling and Blue John caves to visit.

The accommodation has three en suite double rooms, a single and a twin room with shared bathroom. One of the rooms has a four-poster bed.

Nick and Janet Steynberg offer you a hearty Full English, Continental or Vegetarian Breakfast.

A piece of Heaven for you and your family.

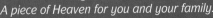

Chinley, Derby

Wi-Fi

Glossop

A warm welcome on the edge of the Peak District

Graham and Julie Caesar

Windy Harbour Farm Hotel

Woodhead Road, Glossop SK13 7QE
01457 853107 • www.peakdistrict-hotel.co.uk
e-mail: enquiries@peakdistrict-hotel.co.uk

Situated in the heart of the Peak District on the B6105, approximately one mile from Glossop town centre and adjacent to the Pennine Way.

All our bedrooms are en suite, with outstanding views of Woodhead and Snake Passes, and the Longdendale Valley is an ideal location for all outdoor activities.

A warm welcome awaits you in our licensed bar and restaurant serving a wide range of excellent home-made food.

Bed and Breakfast from £30 per night

MONA VILLAS
Church Lane
Middle Mayfield
Mayfield
Near Ashbourne
DE6 2JS

*A warm, friendly welcome to our home with
purpose-built en suite accommodation.
Beautiful views over open countryside. A local pub serves
excellent food within a five minute walk.
Situated near Alton Towers, Dove Dale, etc.
Three en suite rooms available, single supplement applies.
Family rooms available. Ground floor rooms.
Rooms have colour TV and tea and coffee facilities.
Full English breakfast.
No smoking. Parking.
An ideal area for walking and mountain biking.*
Bed and Breakfast from £28.00 to £35.00 per night

Tel: 01335 343773
e-mail: info@mona-villas.fsnet.co.uk
www.mona-villas.fsnet.co.uk

Mrs Jane Ball
Brae Cottage
East Bank, Winster DE4 2DT
Tel: 01629 650375

In one of the most picturesque villages in the Peak District National Park
this 300-year-old cottage offers independent accommodation across the
paved courtyard. Breakfast is served in the cottage. Rooms are furnished
and equipped to a high standard; both having en suite shower rooms,
tea/coffee making facilities, TV and heating.

The village has two traditional pubs which provide food.

Local attractions include village (National Trust) Market House, Chatsworth,
Haddon Hall and many walks from the village in the hills and dales.

**Ample private parking • Non-smoking throughout
Bed and Breakfast from £60 per double room**

Leicestershire & Rutland

Barton-Upon-Humber

Lincolnshire

We welcome you to our small, friendly, family-run farmhouse in the delightful hamlet of Deepdale, to enjoy the comfort of our home and garden. Our rooms have en suite or private bathroom, tea/coffee making facilities, TV, radio and hairdryer. Trouser press, iron and board, wet outdoor clothes drying facilities available. We offer the 'Great British' breakfast, with fresh, locally sourced produce where possible; vegetarian and other diets as requested.

We are central for visiting Hull, Beverley, Lincoln and York, and close to historic Barton. There is a SSSI, 3 miles away on the Humber Estuary, and we are 200 yards from a bridleway, leading to a network of bridleways and the Viking Way.

Dogs and horses welcome by arrangement. We have plenty of off-road parking.

Terms from £24.00 pppn. Special breaks and long term discounts available.

Mrs. Pam Atkin

West Wold Farmhouse
Deepdale
Barton-upon-Humber
DN18 6ED
Tel: 01652 633293 / 07889 532937
e-mail: pam@westwoldfarmhouse.co.uk
www.westwoldfarmhouse.co.uk

GUEST HOUSE ★★★★

NO SMOKING

Coast or country, the choice is yours for a holiday in Lincolnshire. With award-winning beaches, miles of clean sand, theme parks, kite surfing, jet skiing and seaside nature reserves, there's action, excitement and interests for everyone right along the coast. At Skegness, as well as all the fun on the beach, children will love watching the seals being fed at the seal sanctuary, and the Parrot Zoo nearby. There's a seal sanctuary at Mablethorpe too, and all the fun of the fairground, as well as beach huts to hire if the sun goes behind a cloud. Further north, at Cleethorpes with its wonderful beaches and Pleasure Island, take a ride on the Cleethorpes Coast Light Railway, or a guided tour of the sand dunes and saltmarshes at the Discovery Centre to find out about local wildlife habitats.

Peterborough

Northamptonshire

Northamptonshire may appear a quiet, rural county, but it's very much a place for action and family fun. Everything you would expect to find in the countryside is here – walking, cycling, fishing, wildlife, castles and stately homes steeped in history, beautiful villages and traditional inns and pubs. As well as all this motorsports enthusiasts will be more than satisfied, with stock car racing at the Northampton International Raceway, Santa Pod, the home of European Drag Racing and the Silverstone circuit. For shoppers, Northampton, the home of high quality footwear in Britain, is still a good place for bargains as well as bespoke shoes, and for some fun, why not end the holiday with a visit to Wicksteed Park at Kettering where you'll find all the family could want in events and entertainment.

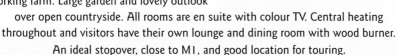

Nottinghamshire

Willow House Bed and Breakfast

SB

A period house (1857) in quiet village
two minutes' walk from beautiful river bank,
yet only five miles from City. Attractive,
interesting accommodation with authentic
Victorian ambience. En suite available.
Bright, clean rooms with tea/coffee facilities, TV.
Off-road parking. Porch for smokers.
Ideally situated for Holme Pierrepont International
Watersports Centre; golf; National Ice Centre;
Trent Bridge (cricket); Sherwood Forest; Nottingham
Racecourse; and the unspoiled historic town of
Southwell with its Minster and Racecourse.
Good local eating. Please phone first for directions.
Rates: From £26 per person per night.

**Mrs V. Baker, Willow House,
Burton Joyce NG14 5FD
Tel:0115 931 2070; Mob: 07816 347706
www.willowhousebedandbreakfast.co.uk**

Dalestorth Guest House is an 18th century Georgian family home converted in the
19th century to become a school for young ladies of the local gentry and a boarding school until the

1930s. In 1976 it was bought by the present owners and
has been modernised and converted into a comfortable,
clean and pleasant guest house serving the areas of
Mansfield and Sutton-in-Ashfield, offering overnight
accommodation of Bed and Breakfast or longer stays to
businessmen, holidaymakers or friends and relations
visiting the area. From £20 per person per night.

**Mr P. Jordan, Dalestorth Guest House,
Skegby Lane, Skegby,
Sutton-in-Ashfield NG17 3DH
Tel: 01623 551110 • Fax: 01623 442241
www.dalestorth.co.uk**

Elton, Mansfield

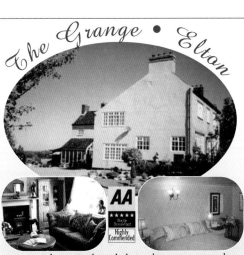

Burghill, Ledbury

Herefordshire

the Heron House, Herefordshire.
- Bed & Breakfast -

Canon Pyon Road, Portway, Burghill, Hereford HR4 8NG
Tel: 01432 761111 • Fax: 01432 760603
e-mail: info@theheronhouse.com • www.theheronhouse.com

Heron House, with its panoramic views of the Malvern Hills, provides friendly and spacious B&B.

Hereford Room: Large double room with rural views, tea/coffee, television. En suite facilities with power shower and toilet.

Gloucester Room: Comfortable twin-bedded room with hot and cold vanity unit, tea/coffee, television. Separate guest bathroom with bath, shower and toilet.

Your Full English Breakfast is served in our relaxing breakfast room.

Please note, we have a no pets and non-smoking policy. Car parking is provided in our secure off-road parking. Unsuitable for lorries and large vehicles.
Situated four miles north of Hereford in a rural location, this is an ideal base for walking, fishing, golf, cycling and bird-watching.

Bed and full English Breakfast from £29 pppn.

SB

The Coach House an eighteenth century coaching stable providing unique Bed & Breakfast accommodation near Ledbury. All around is wonderful walking country, from the Malvern Hills to the Black Mountains. In the main house, guests have sole use of a lounge and kitchen, with a choice of single, double and twin rooms, all en suite. For that special romantic weekend try the *Tower Suite* of private lounge with balcony and en suite double bedroom.

Tariffs: £56 per room per night double and twin, £35 single.
Reduced by £3 per room per night for 3 nights and more.

Tower Suite: min. 2 nights:
£150 for 2 nights and £60 per night thereafter.

Mrs S.W. Born, The Coach House, Putley, Near Ledbury HR8 2QP (01531 670684)
e-mail: info@bandbherefordshire.com   www.bandbherefordshire.com

Ledbury, Ross-on-Wye

Ross-on-Wye

Weobley

Mellington House

Mellington House is a 16thC house in the black-and-white timbered village of Weobley, within easy reach of Hereford and the Welsh Border.

Our B&B apartments are comfortably furnished with excellent amenities. All have tea and coffee making facilities and their own front door. Accommodation comprises twin and double rooms with private / en suite bath or shower room; separate sitting room with TV/DVD/CD. Free wi-fi internet access is also available. A full English breakfast is served every day.

Chris & Alison Saunders, Mellington House, Broad Street, Weobley, Herefordshire HR4 8SA
Tel: 01544 318537 • www.mellingtonhouse.co.uk • info@mellingtonhouse.co.uk

Shropshire

Church Stretton

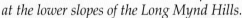

Malt House Farm

Olde worlde beamed farmhouse situated amidst spectacular scenery at the lower slopes of the Long Mynd Hills.

We are a working farm producing beef cattle and sheep. One double bedroom and one twin, both with en suite bathroom, hairdryer and tea tray. Good farmhouse cooking is served in the dining room.

Private guests' sitting room.

- *Non-smoking • Regret no children or pets*
- *Bed and Breakfast from £29.50pppn*

Malt House Farm, Lower Wood,
Church Stretton SY6 6LF
Tel: 01694 751379 • Proprietor: Mrs Lyn Bloor

Church Stretton, Ludlow

SB

Wi-Fi

Staffordshire

Stafford

SB

Wi-Fi

Wyndale Guest House

199 Corporation Street,
Stafford ST16 3LQ
Tel: 01785 223069
wyndale@aol.com
www.wyndaleguesthouse.co.uk

We offer excellent quality accommodation in a quiet yet convenient location, around ten minutes from Stafford town centre, with easy access to the M6. We have eight guest rooms, some en suite, with a range of single, double, twin and family rooms, all with Freeview TV and DVD player. Free internet access. Choice of breakfast, including cereals, porridge, oat cakes, full English breakfast and a selection of home made jams & marmalades plus yogurts & fruits. We also offer specialist diets. Dogs welcome.

Off-road parking and secure storage for bicycles. Close by is a range of shops, pubs, clubs and restaurants, and we are well placed for exploring the many attractions Staffordshire has to offer.

Warwickshire

Kenilworth

Wi-Fi

A comfortable Victorian house close to the town centre and a pleasant stroll from Kenilworth Castle. A market town with excellent restaurants, located in the heart of the Warwickshire countryside, Kenilworth is well connected by road and convenient for the NEC, Stoneleigh Park and the University of Warwick. You'll find the Hollyhurst perfect as a business base or holiday stopover. In either case we offer real hospitality and home comforts in our well equipped guest house. All rooms have en suite/private facilities and there is private parking for up to five vehicles.

Hollyhurst
GUEST HOUSE

AA
★★★
Guest Accommodation

Wi-Fi • No pets
B&B from £36 Single
£58 Double/Twin

**Trudi and Ken Wheat, The Hollyhurst Guest House,
47 Priory Road, Kenilworth CV8 1LL
Tel: 01926 853882
e-mail: admin@hollyhurstguesthouse.co.uk
www.hollyhurstguesthouse.co.uk**

Stratford-Upon-Avon

SB

Wi-Fi

Birmingham

West Midlands

The Awentsbury Hotel

🐴
🐕
SB

Wi-Fi

A Victorian Country House Hotel set in its own grounds in peaceful surroundings, close to Birmingham University, QE Hospital and Cadburys World. Only 2 miles from Birmingham City Centre, the NIA, ICC, the University of Central Birmingham, Aston University and the Bull Ring. Easy Access to the NEC.

- 5 minute walk to Birmingham University.
- Cooked English breakfast and cereals included.
- Vintage cars to view.
- Free Wi-Fi internet throughout hotel.
- Flat screen digital TVs in all rooms.
- Tea and coffee making facilities in rooms.

A warm welcome awaits you.

21 Serpentine Road, Selly Park, Birmingham B29 7HU
Tel: 0121 472 1258
e-mail: ian@awentsbury.com • www.awentsbury.com

---

symbols 🐕🐴SB♿️♀Wi-Fi

🐕	Pets Welcome	🐴	Children Welcome
SB	Short Breaks	♿️	Suitable for Disabled Guests
♀	Licensed	Wi-Fi	Wi-Fi available

Wolverhampton

Featherstone Farm Hotel

New Road, Featherstone, Wolverhampton WV10 7NW

SB
Wi-Fi

A small, high-class country house hotel set in five acres of unspoiled countryside, only one mile from Junction 11 on the M6 or Junction 1 on the M54. The main house has nine en suite bedrooms with all the facilities one would expect in a hotel of distinction. Kings Repose Indian Restaurant, serving freshly prepared dishes, and licensed bar. Secure car park.

• Self-contained fully furnished cottages with maid service are also available.

Tel: 01902 725371 • Fax: 01902 731741

Mobile: 07836 315258

e-mail: featherstonefarmhotel@yahoo.co.uk

www.featherstonefarmhotel.co.uk

Droitwich Spa

Worcestershire

Worcestershire, stretching south-east from the fringes of Birmingham, is a county of Georgian towns, Cotswold stone villages and a Victorian spa, all centred on the cathedral city of Worcester. To the north canals were cut to satisfy the need for transport that grew with industrialisation, and now provide a wonderful opportunity for a leisurely break on a narrowboat, or take a restful look at the countryside from the Severn Valley Railway between Bromsgrove and Kidderminster. Long distance trails like the 100-mile Millenium Way cross the countryside in all directions, or follow one of the many shorter local circular walks. In the Malvern Hills choose between gentle and more strenuous exercise to appreciate the wonderful views of the surrounding countryside, or for a different kind of challenge, try mountain boarding in the hills near Malvern.

Eckington, Great Malvern

Malvern Wells, Worcester

BRICKBARNS, a 200-acre mixed farm, is situated two miles from Great Malvern at the foot of the Malvern Hills, 300 yards from the bus service and one-and-a half miles from the train. The house, which is 300 years old, commands excellent views of the Malvern Hills and guests are accommodated in one double, one single and one family bedrooms with washbasins; two bathrooms, shower room, two toilets; sittingroom and diningroom.

Children welcome and cot and babysitting offered. Central heating. Car essential, parking.

Open Easter to October for Bed and Breakfast from £22 nightly per person. Reductions for children and Senior Citizens.

Birmingham 40 miles, Hereford 20, Gloucester 17, Stratford 35 and the Wye Valley is just 30 miles.

Mrs J.L. Morris, Brickbarns Farm, Hanley Road, Malvern Wells WR14 4HY
Tel: 016845 61775 • Fax: 01886 830037

MOSELEY FARM
BED AND BREAKFAST

SB

Moseley Road, Hallow,
Worcester WR2 6NL
Tel: 01905 64134

Spacious 17th Century former farmhouse with countryside views. Rural location four miles from Worcester City Centre, providing relaxed and comfortable accommodation.

Room only or full English breakfast, from £25pppn.
Large comfortable rooms - three family rooms
(two en suite) and one standard twin. Colour Freeview TV, radio alarm clocks, tea/coffee making facilities and free wifi.
Use of microwave, fridge and toaster.
Pets welcome at no additional charge

e-mail: moseleyfarmbandb@aol.com
www.moseleyfarmbandb.co.uk

East Yorkshire

Bridlington

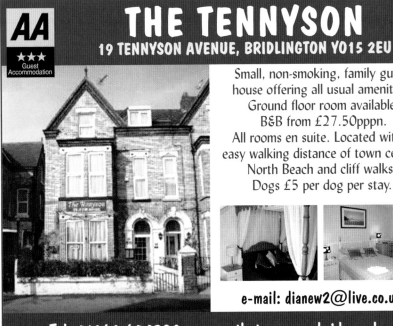

North Yorkshire

Carperby

Danby

Goathland, Harrogate

Dominated by the magnificent York Minster, the largest medieval Gothic cathedral in northern Europe, the city of York in North Yorkshire is full of attractions for the visitor. Have fun finding your way through the Snickelways, the maze of hidden alleyways, and enjoy a morning – or longer – in the array of independent shops and boutiques as well as all the top high street stores. Explore York's past at Jorvik, the recreation of the original Viking city from 1000 years ago or become an archaeologist for the day at Dig! and excavate for yourself items from Viking, Roman, medieval and Victorian times. Outside the city the vast open stretches of the North York Moors and Yorkshire Dales National Parks and the golden sandy beaches of the coast are perfect for an active holiday.

Harrogate, Helmsley

Helmsley

symbols ♞ SB & ♍ Wi-Fi

♞	*Pets Welcome*	♘	*Children Welcome*
SB	*Short Breaks*	♿	*Suitable for Disabled Guests*
♍	*Licensed*	**Wi-Fi**	*Wi-Fi available*

THE OLD STAR
West Witton, Leyburn
DL8 4LU
Tel: 01969 622949
enquiries@theoldstar.com
www.theoldstar.com

Formerly a 17th century coaching inn, now a family-run guest house, you are always welcome at the Old Star.

The building still retains many original features. Comfortable lounge with oak beams and log fire. Well equipped bedrooms, mostly en suite. Delicious, locally sourced Yorkshire breakfast.

Two good food pubs in village. In the heart of the Yorkshire Dales National Park we are ideally situated for walking and touring the Dales. Large car park. Open all year except Christmas.

En suite Bed and Breakfast from £30 pppn.

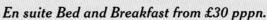

Lovesome Hill Farm
Mary & John Pearson
Tel: 01609 772311
Lovesome Hill,
Northallerton DL6 2PB

Central location for exploring the Dales and Moors, Durham and York. Enjoy the comfort and welcome we have to offer you at our traditional working farm with en suite bedrooms of various combinations and styles, some on ground floor. Gate Cottage, our luxurious suite, with its antique half-tester bed and its own patio, has views towards the Hambleton Hills. Enjoy home-made produce including our own free-range eggs cooked on the Aga. Brochure available.

Seasonal breaks incl. Lambing & Apple Juicing.
Open all year except Christmas and New Year
*B&B from £36-£42 twin/double,
£40-£50 single.
Evening Meal available £15-£20.*

www.lovesomehillfarm.co.uk
e-mail: lovesomehillfarm@btinternet.com

Malham

Malham • Miresfield Farm

SB

- In beautiful gardens bordering village green and stream.
  - Well known for excellent food.
  - 11 bedrooms, all with private facilities.

Mr C. Sharp, Miresfield Farm, Malham, Skipton BD23 4DA • Tel: 01729 830414
www.miresfield-farm.com

- Full central heating.
- Two well furnished lounges and conservatory for guests' use.
- B&B from £32pppn.

Pickering

Wi-Fi

Banavie
Bed & Breakfast

Holiday Accommodation in Thornton-Le-Dale, Pickering, Yorkshire

A large semi-detached house set in a quiet part of the picturesque village of Thornton-le-Dale, one of the prettiest villages in Yorkshire with its famous thatched cottage and bubbling stream flowing through the centre.

We offer our guests a quiet night's sleep and rest away from the main road, yet only four minutes' walk from the village centre.

One large double or twin bedroom and two double bedrooms, all tastefully decorated with en suite facilities, colour TV, hairdryer, shaver point etc. and tea/coffee making facilities. There is a large guest lounge, tea tray on arrival. A real Yorkshire breakfast is served in the dining room.

Places to visit include Castle Howard, Eden Camp, North Yorkshire Moors Railway, Goathland ("Heartbeat"), York etc. There are three pubs, a bistro and a fish and chip shop for meals. Children and dogs welcome. Own keys. Car parking at back of house.

B&B from £30pppn • No Smoking
Welcome To Excellence
SAE please for brochure • Mrs Ella Bowes

BANAVIE, ROXBY ROAD, THORNTON-LE-DALE, PICKERING YO18 7SX
Tel: 01751 474616
e-mail: info@banavie.uk.com   www.banavie.uk.com

SB

One twin and one double en suite rooms, one single with private bathroom; all with tea/coffee making facilities and TV; alarm clock/radio and hairdryer also provided; diningroom; central heating.

ETC ★★★★

Very clean and comfortable accommodation with good food. Situated in a quiet part of this picturesque village, which is in a good position for Moors, countryside, coast, North York Moors Railway, Flamingo Park Zoo and Dalby forest drives, mountain biking and walking. Good facilities for meals provided in the village. Open Easter to October for Bed and Breakfast from £32-£36pp. Private car park. Secure motorbike and cycle storage.

Tangalwood

Roxby Road, Thornton-le-Dale, Pickering YO18 7TQ

TELEPHONE: **01751 474688**

Farfields Farm

SB

Wi-Fi

Peacefully situated working farm overlooking beautiful Newton Dale. Four comfortable ground floor rooms in a lovely old converted character barn just opposite the farmhouse. All rooms are en suite, either twin or super-king, and have digital/DVD TV, beverage tray, fridge and microwave. Delicious farmhouse breakfast using locally sourced produce. Ideal central location for exploring moors, coast and York. Dalby Forest only one mile away. Marvellous walking and bird watching from the farm. Fantastic views of the steam train in the valley below. Inn serving excellent meals only a short stroll away. Tariff £38-£45pppn. Single £50-£60. Special weekly rates.

Mrs E. Stead, Farfields Farm, Lockton, Pickering YO18 7NQ • Tel: 01751 460239 e-mail: stay@farfieldsfarm.co.uk www.farfieldsfarm.co.uk

Mrs Julie Bailes, CHERRY CROFT, Bedale Lane, Wath, Ripon HG4 5ER

SB

- CHERRY CROFT is situated in the quiet village of Wath, approx. three miles north of the historic market town of Ripon; two miles from A1(M).
- Accommodation comprises two double rooms with TV and tea making facilities.
- All rooms are on the ground floor.
- Ideal location for touring the Dales and Herriot Country.
- *From £20 per person, Bed & Breakfast.*

Tel: 01765 640318

Little Pastures · Scarborough

SB

Situated in a beautiful location with panoramic views over the surrounding National Park and sea, and a lovely view of Scarborough Castle; Scarborough's many seaside attractions are only five miles away. Many lovely villages in this beautiful and historic area such as Robin Hood's Bay, Goathland (Heartbeat), Staithes (Captain Cook) are just a car drive away, as well as Whitby (Dracula) Filey and York.

One twin/one double rooms en suite, each with their own private lounge,
TV/DVD/Radio/CD,
tea/coffee and fridge.
Ground floor room with three views.
Ample private parking.
Prices from £30.

Joan & Ron Greenfield, Little Pastures, Hood Lane, Cloughton, Scarborough, North Yorkshire YO13 0AT • Phone: 01723-870564
e-mail: joanrongreenfield@yahoo.co.uk

Scarborough

Scarborough

Harmony Country Lodge

SB

Wi-Fi

Distinctively Different Peaceful and relaxing retreat, octagonal in design and set in two acres of private grounds with 360° panoramic views of the National Park and sea. An ideal centre for walking or touring. Two miles from Scarborough and within easy reach of Whitby, York and the beautiful North Yorkshire countryside. Tastefully decorated en suite centrally heated rooms with colour TV and all with superb views. Attractive dining room, guest lounge and relaxing conservatory. Traditional English breakfast, including vegetarian. Licensed. Private parking facilities. Personal service and warm, friendly Yorkshire hospitality.

• *Bed and Breakfast from £28 to £40.75. Non-smoking. Children over 7 years welcome* •
• *Spacious 5-berth caravan also available for self-catering holidays – £150 to £350* •

Sue and Tony Hewitt, Harmony Country Lodge, Limestone Road, Burniston, Scarborough YO13 0DG • 0800 2985840 • Tel & Fax: 01723 870276 e-mail: mail@harmonylodge.net • www.harmonycountrylodge.co.uk

Plane Tree Cottage Farm
•• Bed & Breakfast ••
Staintondale, Scarborough YO13 0EY
Tel: 01723 870796 • Mrs M. Edmondson

This small mixed farm is situated off the beaten track, with open views of beautiful countryside and the sea. Many guests return year after year to enjoy a peaceful, relaxing, away-from-it-all holiday.

Excellent breakfasts using eggs from the farm's free-range hens and homemade bread.

Well equipped rooms, one on the ground floor, own lounge and separate dining room.

Sorry no dogs. Minimum 2 nights' stay. Closed November to February inclusive.

Special rate for longer stays. Car essential.

Staintondale is about half-way between Scarborough and Whitby and near the North York Moors. An ideal holiday for anyone wanting peace and quiet.
Within easy reach of North York Moors Railway, Goathland, Whitby and York.
Caravan accommodation also available
More details on request.

Staithes, Thirsk, Thornton-le-Dale

SB
♿
Wi-Fi

HALL FARM
Gilling East, York YO62 4JW
e-mail: virginia@hallfarmgilling.co.uk
www.hallfarmgilling.co.uk
01439 788314

Come and stay with us at Hall Farm

A beautifully situated 470-acre working stock farm with extensive views over Ryedale.

We offer a friendly, family welcome with home made scones on arrival. A ground floor double en suite room is available, with TV and hospitality tray with home-made biscuits. Sittingroom with open fire on chilly evenings. Breakfast is served in the conservatory. Full English Breakfast includes home-made bread and preserves and locally sourced produce.

Terms from £35 per person.

**Excellent eating places in Helmsley and the nearby villages.
York, Castle Howard and the North York Moors within half-an-hour drive.**

SB

Diana and John offer all their guests a friendly and warm welcome to their Victorian end town house a few minutes' walk from the city centre, York's beautiful Minster, medieval walls and museums. We are only a 40 mile drive from coastal resorts, the lovely Yorkshire Moors and Dales.

Three double/twin en suite rooms, colour TV, tea/coffee tray, central heating • Breakfast menu • Car park. NON-SMOKING • Fire Certificate • Terms from £26pp.

Newton House

Newton House, Neville Street, Haxby Road, York YO31 8NP • 01904 635627

West Yorkshire

If you are looking for a warm and comfortable environment in which to relax and enjoy your stay whilst visiting Yorkshire then The Manor will be perfect for you. This luxurious 5 Star Gold Award retreat offers a relaxing and refreshing base from which to explore some of the most beautiful countryside in Yorkshire. Lovingly restored, this 18th Century Manor House is enhanced by many original features. Ideally situated for exploring the rugged Pennine moorland or Bronte Country, the Yorkshire Dales and beyond.

SB

Wi-Fi

- Ample off-road car parking
- Centrally heated en suite rooms
- Welcome tray with homemade biscuits
- Top quality beds and linen
- Satellite TV with DVD player
- Wi-Fi Internet access
- Extensive DVD library
- Hairdryer, CD player & radio alarm clock
- Easy access to all major attractions
- Debit & credit cards accepted
- Private guest lounge
- Thick fluffy towels
- Extensive complimentary toiletries
- Iron & ironing board available
- Packed lunches available on request
- Hearty Yorkshire breakfast menu

The Manor Guest House
Sutton Drive, Cullingworth, Bradford BD13 5BQ
Tel: 01535 274374
e-mail: info@cullingworthmanor.co.uk
www.cullingworthmanor.co.uk

•••Heath House•••

An elegant Victorian house set in 4 acres. All en suite rooms are comfortably furnished with TV, tea/coffee tray. Breakfast, which is served in the dining hall, is freshly cooked to order. Wheelchair access to ground floor bedrooms. Children welcome. Well behaved pets welcome. Parking. Open all year. Easy drive to Leeds, Bradford and Dewsbury.

Chancery Road, Ossett, Wakefield WF5 9RZ • 01924 260654
bookings@heath-house.co.uk • www.heath-house.co.uk

Durham

If you're looking for a few days' break somewhere different, why not go to the city of Durham? Set between the North Pennines and the Durham Heritage Coast, the old medieval heart with its cobbled streets is dominated by the cathedral and castle, a World Heritage Site, and a must for visitors. On the way back to the modern shopping centre, browse through individual boutiques and galleries in the alleys and vennels, and the stalls of the Victorian market, then enjoy a stroll along the riverside walks. Stay for longer in County Durham, tour all the heritage sites and enjoy invigorating walks and hikes through the dramatic Pennines countryside and along the clifftop path at the coast. There are paths, trails and tracks for all standards of fitness, whether a family ramble and picnic or a hike along the Pennine Way. High Force, the highest waterfall in England, on the Raby Castle estate, is easily accessible.

Alnmouth

Northumberland

Rambling over the heather-clad Cheviot moorlands, exploring the castles and pele towers built to ward off invading Scots, watching the feast of wildlife on the coast and in the countryside, breathing in the wonderful sea air on a golden sandy beach, you'll find it all in Northumberland. On the coast, a designated Area of Outstanding Natural Beauty, keen walkers can take the Coast Path from the walled Georgian market town of Berwick-on-Tweed to Cresswell, stopping at little fishing villages on the way. Follow the section along Embleton beach from Craster, best known for its traditionally smoked kippers, to get the best views of the ruins of Dunstanburgh Castle. At the lively market town of Alnwick visit the castle, Hogwarts in the Harry Potter films, with its redeveloped gardens, magnificent water features and even a poison garden!

Redfoot Lea

SB

Part of a recently converted farmsteading dating back to 1850. On the outskirts of Alnwick (1.5 miles), the house has the advantage of being in the country, while being close to local amenities and attractions, bars and restaurants. There are two cosy, co-ordinated, well equipped bedrooms on the ground floor, a beautiful sitting room with a south-facing aspect, and a spectacular dining hall. Open all year.

North Northumberland Local Food 'Gold Award'.

Greensfield Moor Farm, Alnwick NE66 2HH
Tel: 01665 603891•Fax: 01665 606429•Mobile: 07870 586214
info@redfootlea.co.uk • www.redfootlea.co.uk

❖ Struthers Farm ❖

Catton, Allendale, Hexham NE47 9LP

Struthers Farm offers a warm welcome in the heart of England, with
many splendid local walks from the farm itself. Panoramic views.
Situated in an area of outstanding beauty. Double/twin rooms,
en suite bathrooms, central heating. Good farmhouse cooking.
Ample safe parking. Come and share our home and enjoy
beautiful countryside. Near Hadrian's Wall (½ hour's drive).

Children welcome, pets by prior
arrangement. Open all year.

Bed and Breakfast from £30;
Optional Evening Meal
from £12.50.

Contact Mrs Ruby Keenleyside
01434 683580
www.struthersfarmbandb.com

Waren House Hotel

Set in six acres of mature wooded grounds,
Waren House has been reborn under the talented and loving
hands of owners, Anita and Peter Laverack,
and offers today's visitor a rare retreat for true relaxation,
along with a central point for venturing through the delights of
North Northumberland and the Scottish Borders.

Breakfast and dinner are served in the beautiful and romantic
dining room where food is presented with the utmost care.
Our cellar is stocked with a huge choice of reasonably priced
fine wines. All public rooms and bedrooms are non-smoking.

Relax in the gardens or in the comfortable lounge and adjacent library. For those seeking the
simple pleasures of walking - the sandy shore offers mile upon mile of beautiful scenery.

From this tranquil setting it is easy to find the treasures of the Heritage Coast, including the
magnificent castle at Bamburgh, just two miles away.

Waren Mill, Belford, Near Bamburgh, Northumberland NE70 7EE
Tel: 01668 214581 • Fax: 01668 214484
e-mail: enquiries@warenhousehotel.co.uk
www.warenhousehotel.co.uk

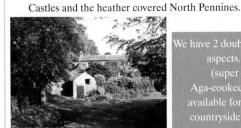

Hexham

SB

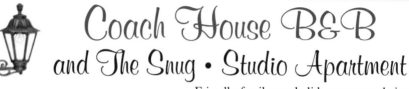

SB

Wi-Fi

The Anglers Arms

A Legend in the very Heart of Northumberland

SB

Wi-Fi

This traditional Coaching Inn is situated only 6 miles from Morpeth, beside picturesque Weldon Bridge on the River Coquet. Bedrooms are cosy and welcoming, with a touch of olde worlde charm. Be prepared for a hearty Northumbrian breakfast! Meals can be be enjoyed in the friendly bar, or outdoors on sunny summer days; alternatively dine in style and sophistication in the à la carte Pullman Railway Carriage restaurant. Ideal for exploring both coast and country, the Inn also caters for fishermen, with its own one-mile stretch of the River Coquet available free to residents.

The Anglers Arms, Weldon Bridge, Longframlington, Northumberland NE65 8AX

Tel: 01665 570271/570655 • Fax: 01665 570041
e-mail: info@anglersarms.com • www.anglersarms.com

Hospitality, comfort and simply breathtaking views set the atmosphere for your visit to Dunns Houses. Welcome to our farmhouse, built in the 1400s in Border Reiver country, on a 960 acre stock farm in an Area of Outstanding Natural Beauty. Panoramic views of the Rede Valley and the Cheviot Hills. Private fishing for brown trout and salmon. Lockup garage for cycles and boiler house for walkers' clothing and boots.

SB

Wi-Fi

Many activities available close by including golf, cycling and walking on the Pennine Way, as well as Kielder Water and Forest for all sorts of outdoor activities and water sports. Spacious en suite bedrooms and guests' lounge in self-contained part of our home with fantastic views of the Rede Valley, Otterburn and the foothills of the Cheviots. TV, snooker/pool table, games and rocking horses for the younger children. Tasty, pre-booked evening meals; breakfast using good quality local bacon, sausage and eggs. Open all year. Children and pets welcome. Terms from £35 twin/double, £45 single.

Mrs Jane Walton, Dunns Houses, Otterburn,
Newcastle Upon Tyne NE19 1LB
01830 520677 • 07808 592701
e-mail: dunnshouses@hotmail.com
www.northumberlandfarmholidays.co.uk

AA
★★★★
Farmhouse

SB

Wi-Fi

Glimpse the red squirrel from our splendid 18th century Georgian farmhouse on this 1100 acre livestock farm. Relax in beautifully appointed, spacious en suite bedrooms with superb views over open countryside. Elegant, comfortable lounge with log fire. Delicious Aga cooked breakfasts using local produce, with home-made bread and preserves.

Ideally located for visiting Northumberland's many attractions including Alnwick Castle and Gardens and National Trust Cragside.

- *'Pride of Northumbria' Best B&B Award Winner*
- *Open March-November*
- *Children welcome*
- *Terms from £40 twin/double, £55 single.*

Lee Farm, Near Rothbury,
Longframlington, Morpeth NE65 8JQ
Contact: Mrs Susan Aynsley
Tel & Fax: 01665 570257
e-mail: enqs@leefarm.co.uk
www.leefarm.co.uk

Katerina's Guest House

SB

Wi-Fi

High Street, Rothbury NE65 7TQ • 01669 620691

Charming old guest house, ideally situated for the amenities of pretty Rothbury village, and to explore Northumberland's hills, coast, Alnwick Castle and gardens. Beautiful bedrooms, each decorated and colour co-ordinated to enhance its individual character; some with original stone fireplaces/beamed ceilings, all en suite, with four-poster beds, TV, and superbly stocked tea tray. Free Wi-Fi. Wide, interesting choice of breakfasts; licensed evening meals also available – sample Cath's bread, 'whisky porridge', vegetarian nutballs, or Steak Katerina.

Bed and Breakfast from £68-£78 per room per night, depending on number of nights booked.

e-mail: ian.mills6@btopenworld.com
www.katerinasguesthouse.co.uk

Wyndgrove House

Bed & Breakfast Accommodation on the Northumberland coast

Welcome to Wyndgrove House in the pretty North Northumberland village of Seahouses.
10 minutes' walk from the beaches and the harbour, in a quiet leafy conservation area.
Light large rooms are perfect for relaxing; the spacious bedrooms feature king-size beds
with pure Egyptian cotton bed linen and generous bath sheets. Hospitality trays are well
stocked with quality Fair Trade products and biscuits. Breakfast is served in our light,
sunny, south-facing dining room where a freshly cooked breakfast of the best local
produce will set you up for the day. Ideal base for exploring this scenic area.

**156 Main Street, Seahouses,
Northumberland NE68 7UA
Telephone: 01665 720 767**
e-mail: wyndgrovehouse@gmail.com
www.wyndgrovehouse.co.uk

THE OLDE SHIP INN

Main Street,
Seahouses,
Northumberland
NE68 7RD
Tel: 01665 720200
Fax: 01665 721383

A former farmhouse dating
from 1745, the inn stands
overlooking the harbour in
the village of Seahouses.

SB
Wi-Fi

The Olde Ship, first licensed in 1812, has been in the same family for over
100 years and is now a fully residential inn. All guest rooms, including three
with four-poster beds, and executive suites with lounges and sea views, are
en suite, with television, refreshment facilities, direct-dial telephone and
Wi-Fi. The bars and corridors bulge at the seams with nautical memorabilia.
Good home cooking features locally caught seafood, along with soups,
puddings and casseroles.

www.seahouses.co.uk • e-mail: theoldeship@seahouses.co.uk

Wooler

East Horton Farmhouse
BED & BREAKFAST

East Horton is situated between the market town of Wooler and the coastal village of Belford in the most historic and beautiful corner of Northumberland. It has stunning views south down the valley towards Alnwick and west to the Cheviot Hills.

Recently refurbished to a very high standard, our three en suite guest bedrooms are south facing, spacious and well appointed with TVs, hospitality trays, hairdryers etc. All food is sourced locally and we use free range and organic produce whenever possible.

East Horton, Wooler, Northumberland NE71 6EZ • Tel: 01668 215 216
e-mail: sed@hazelrigg.fsnet.co.uk • www.farmhousebandb.co.uk

Bestselling holiday accommodation guides for over 65 years

Visit the FHG website
www.holidayguides.com
for all kinds of holiday accommodation in Britain

Balterley, Chester

Cheshire

Christleton (Chester), Crewe

In Cheshire, just south of Manchester, combine a city break in historic Chester with a day or two at one of relaxing spas either in the city itself or in one of the luxury resorts in the rolling countryside. A round at an on-site golf course offers an alternative way of enjoying the break, and while out in the country, why not visit one of the many gardens open to the public? Chester, with its wonderful array of Roman, medieval and Georgian buildings is a fascinating place to visit. Walk round the most complete example of city walls in the whole country, past the beautiful cathedral, before browsing through the wonderful range of shops, art galleries and museums. Explore the history of the area at the Dewa Roman Experience, with reconstructed Roman streets, and take the opportunity to see the Roman, Saxon and medieval remains on view.

Holmes Chapel, Macclesfield

Nantwich

LEA FARM

Charming farmhouse set in landscaped gardens, where peacocks roam, on 150-acre working family farm. Spacious bedrooms, colour TVs, electric blankets, radio alarm and tea/coffee making facilities. Centrally heated throughout. Family, double and twin bedrooms, en suite facilities. Luxury lounge, dining room overlooking gardens. Pool/snooker; fishing in well stocked pool in beautiful surroundings. Bird watching. Children welcome, also dogs if kept under control. Help feed the birds and animals. *Near to Stapeley Water Gardens, Bridgemere Garden World. Also Nantwich, Crewe, Chester, the Potteries and Alton Towers. B&B from £28pp • children half price.*

Wrinehill Road, Wybunbury, Nantwich CW5 7NS

Tel: 01270 841429

e-mail: leafarm@hotmail.co.uk • www.leafarm.co.uk

Cumbria

The stunning scenery of the region now known as Cumbria, in England's north west, from the Solway Firth in the north to the coasts of Morecambe Bay in the south, the ports and seaside villages in the west to the Pennines in the east, and including the Lake District National Park, has been attracting tourists since the end of the 17th century, and the number of visitors has been increasing ever since. All kinds of outdoor activities are available, from gorge walking and ghyll scrambling to a trek through the countryside on horseback or a quiet afternoon rowing on a tranquil lake. The area is a walkers' paradise, and whether on foot, in a wheelchair or a pushchair there's a path and trail for everyone.

Ambleside

SB

Ambleside

SB

Wi-Fi

SB

Wi-Fi

Ambleside, Appleby-in-Westmorland

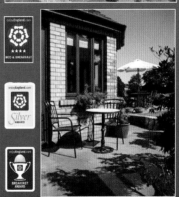

Bowness-on-Windermere, Broughton-in-Furness

Carlisle

ABBERLEY HOUSE

33 Victoria Place, Carlisle CA1 1HP

 SB

Tel: 01228 521645

A charming Victorian Guest House located in the centre of Carlisle offering single, double/ twin and family en suite rooms with flat screen TV, tea and coffee facilities, free Wi-Fi and private parking. We are only a short walk from the city centre with its fine variety of shops, restaurants, pubs and of course the cathedral, castle and award-winning Tullie House museum. Also close by are Stoney Holme and Swift golf courses, the Sands sports and leisure centre and the splendid River Eden.

Wi-Fi

A short drive takes you to historic Hadrian's Wall and the magnificent Lake District; a convenient place to stay over en route to Scotland.

Our rates start from only £30 per person which includes English breakfast and taxes.

e-mail: info@abberleyhouse.co.uk • www.abberleyhouse.co.uk

THE YEWDALE HOTEL • CONISTON

Yewdale Road, Coniston LA21 8DU • Tel: 015394 41280

The Yewdale Hotel is a situated in the centre of Coniston, central for the scenic delights of the Lake District. Accommodation is available in eight centrally heated en suite bedrooms, with TV and tea-making facilities, and an excellent Cumbrian breakfast starts the day. In the bar and dining room fresh seasonal produce features on a varied menu which includes plenty of choice for vegetarians, as well as children's dishes.

Fishing, boating, canoeing, walking and pony trekking are all available on or around Coniston Water, and those with energy to spare can tackle the climb up the 2,600ft Old Man of Coniston. The Ruskin Museum in the village celebrates the life and work of the Victorian artist John Ruskin, and a short ferry trip across the Lake takes visitors to Brantwood, Ruskin's home.

The hotel is open daily for breakfast, morning coffee, snacks, lunches, afternoon tea and evening meals. Non-residents welcome.

info@yewdalehotel.com • www.yewdalehotel.com

Gilsland, Howgill

SB

SB

Maple Bank Country Guest House

Rhona and Tommy extend a warm welcome to guests both old and new at Maple Bank Country Guest House, a magnificent Edwardian residence set in an acre of beautiful gardens near the town of Keswick, right in the heart of the Lake District National Park and close to all of its many facilities. The House commands uninterrupted views across the Derwent valley towards the lofty Skiddaw and the smaller Latrigg, and is ideally placed for walking, climbing, water sports, and other less strenuous activities like fishing or visiting local pubs and eateries! We pride ourselves on the service we offer to guests and will try our utmost to make your stay as comfortable and enjoyable as possible.

We have plentiful free and secure parking, secure cycle storage and a drying room.

There are 5 spacious double rooms and two twin rooms, all en suite with colour TV, plentiful wardrobe space, tea & coffee making facilities, iron and ironing board (on request), and hairdryer. Our spacious yet cosy family room is en suite, with one double bed, one single bed, colour TV, plentiful wardrobe space, tea & coffee making facilities, iron and ironing board (on request), and hairdryer

Maple Bank, Braithwaite, Keswick, Cumbria CA12 5RY
Tel: 01768 778229 • Fax: 01768 778000
e-mail: enquiries@maplebank.co.uk • www.maplebank.co.uk

SB

Wi-Fi

The Hollies Guesthouse,
Threlkeld, Keswick,
Cumbria CA12 4RX

The Hollies B&B guesthouse is situated in the centre of Threlkeld village, near Keswick in the English Lake District National Park. The accommodation comprises four twin/double rooms, all with en suite bathrooms. The rooms have full central heating and come with tea/coffee making facilities, television, DVD and free Wi-Fi internet.
Well behaved dogs are welcome by prior arrangement in some of the rooms.
Room rates include a superb Cumbrian breakfast using only the best local produce.
There is ample off-road parking, as well as facilities for both walkers and cyclists (including drying facilities). *Twin/Double from £37pppn. Single occupancy supplement £10.00.*

Tel: 017687 79216 • e-mail: info@theholliesinlakeland.co.uk
www.theholliesinlakeland.co.uk

Keswick

Keswick, Kirkby Stephen

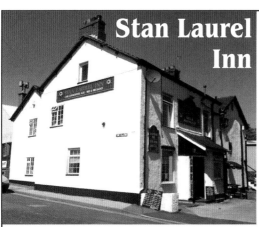

Windermere

Windermere

symbols 🐕🎠SB♿♟Wi-Fi

🐕	Pets Welcome	🎠	Children Welcome
SB	Short Breaks	♿	Suitable for Disabled Guests
♟	Licensed	Wi-Fi	Wi-Fi available

Windermere

Fir Trees

in the heart of the English Lake District

Situated midway between Windermere village and the lake, built in the traditional Lakeland style, Fir Trees offers delightful accommodation of exceptional quality and charm. Our bedrooms are lovely, all furnished and decorated to a very high standard and all have private en suite, tea/coffee making facilities and television. Breakfasts are traditionally English in style and cooked to perfection. Free use of leisure facilities at nearby country club. Plenty of off-road parking.

*Midweek Breaks
Sunday night to Friday morning:
£155 for 3 nights B&B per couple*

**Lake Road, Windermere, Cumbria LA23 2EQ
Tel: 015394 42272 • Fax: 015394 42512
enquiries@fir-trees.co.uk • www.fir-trees.co.uk**

Blackpool

Lancashire

Spending Our Time Making Yours Memorable

SB

Wi-Fi

At the 4 Star multi award-winning Berwick you will receive a warm and friendly welcome, enjoy a relaxing break and experience customer service at its best. Beautifully decorated en suite guest bedrooms, flat screen TVs, comfortable lounge and spacious dining room. Extensive choice of home-made food at breakfast and dinner.

From £25.50pppn B&B, based on two people sharing a room. Evening meal available. Special offers for longer stays.

23 King Edward Avenue, Blackpool FY2 9TA
Tel: 01253 351496
enquiries@theberwickhotel.co.uk
www.theberwickhotel.co.uk

WINNER - Excellence in Customer Care 2008/9 (WTB)
HIGHLY COMMENDED - Excellence in Customer Service 2009 (LETS)

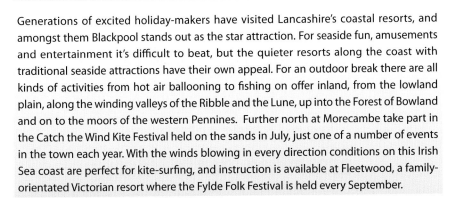

Generations of excited holiday-makers have visited Lancashire's coastal resorts, and amongst them Blackpool stands out as the star attraction. For seaside fun, amusements and entertainment it's difficult to beat, but the quieter resorts along the coast with traditional seaside attractions have their own appeal. For an outdoor break there are all kinds of activities from hot air ballooning to fishing on offer inland, from the lowland plain, along the winding valleys of the Ribble and the Lune, up into the Forest of Bowland and on to the moors of the western Pennines. Further north at Morecambe take part in the Catch the Wind Kite Festival held on the sands in July, just one of a number of events in the town each year. With the winds blowing in every direction conditions on this Irish Sea coast are perfect for kite-surfing, and instruction is available at Fleetwood, a family-orientated Victorian resort where the Fylde Folk Festival is held every September.

Chorley

SB

Wi-Fi

Parr Hall Farm

ETC/AA ★★★★

Within an hour of the Lake District, Yorkshire Dales, Peak District, Chester and North Wales, Parr Hall Farm is an ideal base for touring the local area. Attractions nearby include Camelot Theme Park, Martin Mere, Southport, Blackpool and antiques at Bygone Times, Heskin Hall, Park Hall and Botany Bay. All rooms are en suite, with central heating. Good food nearby. Ground floor rooms. Off-road parking.

From M6 take A5209 for Parbold, then immediately take B5250 right turn for Eccleston. After five miles, Parr Lane is on the right, the house is first on the left.

B&B from £35 per person, reductions for children.

Parr Hall Farm, Eccleston, Chorley PR7 5SL
Tel: 01257 451917
enquiries@parrhallfarm.com • www.parrhallfarm.com

Bestselling holiday accommodation guides for over 65 years

Visit the FHG website
www.holidayguides.com
for all kinds of holiday accommodation in Britain

Anglesey, Criccieth

Anglesey & Gwynedd

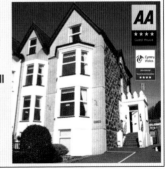

Time, space and freedom to explore beautiful....

North Wales

Minutes from the stunning mountains of Snowdonia and the glorious beaches of Anglesey, North Wales offers an experience unlike any other. Historical landscapes, mythical legends, arts and crafts as well as a taste of the modern; the space to explore them all is in abundance.

Time, space and freedom to explore beautiful... Let the dramatic scenery inspire you while our facilities at Bangor University impress you. With a dedicated team of staff on hand throughout your stay, we have everything you need to ensure your time with us is memorable.

If you're looking for an inspirational location, nature's own adventure playground, or a place to rest your head between activities in North Wales, then...

Join us @ Bangor

We offer:
- Catered individual & group accommodation
- Social functions
- Individually tailored packages
- On site leisure facilities
- Fine dining
- Weddings

Email : conferences@bangor.ac.uk
Web : www.bangor.ac.uk/conferences
Tel : 01248 388088

Tywyn

SB

Eisteddfa

Eisteddfa offers you the comfort of a newly-built bungalow on the Tan-y-coed Ucha Farm, situated adjacent to the farmhouse but with all the benefits of Bed and Breakfast accommodation. The bungalow, which has been designed to accommodate disabled guests, is conveniently situated between Abergynolwyn and Dolgoch Falls with Talyllyn Narrow Gauge Railway running through the farmland. Three bedrooms, two en suite and the third with a shower and washbasin suitable for a disabled person. The toilet is located in the adjacent bathroom. Tea/coffee tray and TV are provided in the bedrooms as are many other extras. We also cater for Coeliac Diets.

Cymru Wales ★★★★

Abergynolwyn, Tywyn LL36 9UP
Mrs Gweniona Pugh • 01654 782385
e-mail: hugh.pugh01@btinternet.com

AA
★★★★
FARMHOUSE

North Wales

Betws-y-Coed

SB

Bron Celyn Guest House, Lôn Muriau, Llanrwst Road,
Betws-y-Coed LL24 0HD • Tel: 01690 710333 • Fax: 01690 710111

A warm welcome awaits you at this delightful guest house overlooking the Gwydyr Forest and Llugwy/Conwy Valleys and village of Betws-y-Coed in Snowdonia National Park. Ideal centre for touring, walking, climbing, fishing and golf. Also excellent overnight stop en route for Holyhead ferries. Easy walk into village and close to Conwy/Swallow Falls and Fairy Glen.

Most rooms en suite, all with colour TV and beverage makers. Lounge. Full central heating. Garden. Car park. Open all year. Full hearty breakfast, packed meals, evening meals - special diets catered for. Walkers and Cyclists Welcome.

B&B from £24 to £35, reduced rates for children under 12 years.
Special out of season breaks.
Jim and Lilian Boughton

Cymru Wales ★★★

e-mail: welcome@broncelyn.co.uk • www.broncelyn.co.uk

Conwy

The Park Hill /Gwesty Bryn Parc
Llanrwst Road, Betws-y-Coed, Conwy LL24 0HD

SB

Wi-Fi

OUR HOME IS YOUR CASTLE. Family-run country guest house. Ideally situated in Snowdonia National Park. Breathtaking views of Conwy/Llugwy Valleys. Renowned for its excellent service and teddy bear collection. Indoor heated swimming pool with sauna free and exclusively for our guests. Secluded free car park. Golf course and village within six minutes' walking distance. Walkers welcome; guided walks on request. Free shuttle service to nearest railway stations. All our rooms with en suite bathroom facilities, coffee/tea tray, Freeview TV etc. Full cooked English Breakfast. Multilingual staff.

Tel: 01690 710540
e-mail: welcome@park-hill.co.uk
www.park-hill.co.uk

Bed and Breakfast from £33pppn

Carmarthenshire

St Clears

Coedllys Uchaf Country House
Llangynin • St. Clears • Carmarthenshire SA33 4JY

Finalist in the AA's Friendliest B&B 2012 Award
Best B&B in Carmarthenshire Award 2012
AA Guest Accommodation of the Year

A beautifully renovated Georgian farmhouse offering superb luxury bed and breakfast accommodation, tucked away in the heart of Carmarthenshire overlooking its own woodland valley and rolling green farmland. Beautiful beaches, coastal paths, Dylan Thomas's Laugharne, Pembrokeshire and Ceredigion are a short drive away.

Our antique queen-size beds are indulgent, comfortable and romantic; the best of linens, soft bath sheets, bathrobes, slippers and pamper baskets make Coedllys even more special.

One well behaved pet welcome; children over 12 years only.

Tel: 01994 231455 • info@coedllyscountryhouse.co.uk
www.coedllyscountryhouse.co.uk

Ceredigion

Cardigan

Pembrokeshire

Haverfordwest

Hay-on-Wye, Welshpool

Powys

Llandrindod Wells, Montgomery

SB

Wi-Fi

Tastefully restored Tudor farmhouse on working farm in peaceful location. En suite bedrooms with breathtaking views over fields and woods, colour TV, beverage trays.

Lounge with log fire. A real taste of Wales in hospitality and cuisine. Wonderful area for wildlife, walking, cycling, near Red Kite feeding station. Safe parking. Brochure on request.

Open all year.

Holly Farm

 Cymru Wales ★★★★

Bed and Breakfast from £32 to £40 per day.

 AA ★★★★ FARMHOUSE

Mrs Ruth Jones, Holly Farm, Howey, Llandrindod Wells LD1 5PP
Tel & Fax: 01597 822402
ruth@hollyfarmbandb.co.uk • www.hollyfarmbandb.co.uk
Taste of Wales Tourism Award • Farm Stay UK Member

SB

Cymru Wales ★★★★

Drewin Farm

A family-run mixed farm set on hillside overlooking panoramic views of the most beautiful countryside. The Drewin is a charming 17th century farmhouse retaining much of its original character with oak beams and large inglenook fireplace, separate lounge; twin and family rooms, both en suite and all modern amenities with colour TV. Full central heating. Offa's Dyke footpath runs through the farm - a wonderful area for wildlife. Ideal base for touring the many beauty spots around. Good home cooking and a very warm welcome await our visitors.

Bed and Breakfast £30pp for one night, £29 for more than one night. Evening Meal by arrangement. Open March to October.

Featured in the BBC Travel Show. Holder of Essential Food Hygiene Certificate and Farmhouse Award from Wales Tourist Board, AA Best Breakfast in Wales Award.

Ceinwen Richards, The Drewin Farm, Churchstoke,
Montgomery SY15 6TW • Tel: 01588 620325
drewinfarm@hotmail.com • www.offasdyke.co.uk/drewinfarm

Cowbridge, Gower Peninsula

South Wales

Montgomery

Aberdeen, Banff & Moray

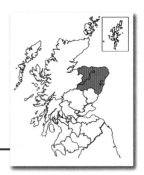

Wi-Fi

Furain Guest House

IDEAL FOR ACCESSING CASTLE AND WHISKY TRAILS AND ROYAL DEESIDE, FISHING, GOLF AND WALKING AVAILABLE LOCALLY.

Furain Guest House, on the A93 8 miles west of Aberdeen centre, is a late Victorian house built from red granite. We have some of the most beautiful countryside in the UK right on our doorstep, offering plenty of scope for walkers. Drum and Crathes Castles are only a few minutes' drive. Golf can be arranged at Peterculter Golf Club, our local course.

•*3 Double rooms* • *2 Family rooms* • *1 Single room* • *2 Twin rooms*
• *Wi-Fi available* • *Children welcome* • *Pets by arrangement*

Contact: Mr Reid,
Furain Guest House,
92 North Deeside Road,
Peterculter,
Aberdeen AB14 0QN
Tel: 01224 732189
Fax: 01224 739070
e-mail: furain@btinternet.com
www.furain.co.uk

Dominated by the Grampian Highlands to the west, extending through Royal Deeside, and with a long coastline along the Moray Firth and the North Sea, Aberdeenshire, Banff and Moray presents a wonderful combination of countryside, coast and heritage for the holidaymaker to explore. Easily accessible from Aberdeen, with all the attractions of city life, this is an ideal corner of the country for an interesting and relaxing break. Why not follow a tourist trail to see the spectacular scenery and learn more about the area at the same time? A visit to this part of Scotland isn't complete without sampling whisky, the national drink, and what better way than to follow the Malt Whisky Trail, visiting distilleries and a traditional cooperage all the way from Forres through the country towns, woodlands and glens of Speyside to remote Glenlivet on the way to the Grampians.

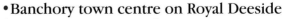

Forres

Argyll & Bute

Ballachulish

The Argyll Arms Hotel, located on the waterfront of the village of Bunessan, and close to the famous Isle of Iona, provides accommodation, bar and restaurant facilities on the beautiful Isle of Mull.

With spectacular sea and island views, the hotel is the perfect base from which to explore, either by car or on foot if walking is your forte, or by bike. We can arrange bike hire or why not bring your own? Secure storage is available and bikers are most welcome. The new owners invite you to enjoy their friendly and relaxed Scottish hospitality in comfortable accommodation, value-for-money bistro-style food and the unique atmosphere of the Isle of Mull. All rooms en suite.

Open all day 365 days of the year catering for residents and non residents.

THE
PALACE HOTEL
OBAN

A small, family hotel offering personal supervision, located on Oban's sea front, with wonderful views over the bay, and less than five minutes' walk from the ferry terminal, train and bus station.

The best view in the bay...

Oban, the "Gateway to the Isles", is the ideal base for a West Highland holiday. By boat you can visit the islands of Kerrera, Coll, Tiree, Lismore, Mull and Iona, and by road Glencoe, Ben Nevis and Inveraray.
Fishing, golf, horse riding, sailing, tennis and bowls all nearby.

Built nearly 100 years ago, the hotel has been tastefully modernised and redecorated, while keeping as many of the original features as possible.

13 en suite individually decorated bedrooms, most with FreeSat and large screen TVs and tea/coffee making facilities. WiFi in public areas and bedrooms.

Breakfast is served in the dining room overlooking the bay. Packed lunches available when requested in advance.

Well behaved pets welcome. Reductions for children.

The Palace Hotel
George Street, Oban, Argyll PA34 5SB
Tel: 01631 562294 • Fax: 01631 562863

www.palacehoteloban.co.uk

SB

Small, family-run guest house where we aim to make your stay as comfortable as possible. All rooms have central heating, colour TV and hospitality trays; some en suite. A full Scottish breakfast is served, although Continental is available if preferred. We have ample private parking at the rear of the house. Situated 10 minutes' walk from the town centre, train, boat and bus terminals. Oban boasts regular sailings to the Islands, and an excellent golf course, as well as walking, cycling, fishing, or just letting the world go by.

A warm welcome awaits you all year round.

MRS STEWART, GLENVIEW, SOROBA ROAD, OBAN PA34 4JF • Tel: 01631 562267
e-mail: morven.stewart@hotmail.co.uk

SB

Wi-Fi

The Falls of Lora Hotel
Connel Ferry, By Oban PA37 1PB
Oban 5 miles, only 2½-3 hours' drive north-west of Glasgow/Edinburgh.

Overlooking Loch Etive, this fine owner-run Victorian hotel with a modern extension offers a warm welcome, good food, service and comfort. 30 bedrooms including 7 luxury rooms (one with four-poster and round bath, another with a 7' round bed and Jacuzzi bathroom), standard twins and doubles, inexpensive family rooms with bunk beds. Relax in the lochside garden across the road, or in the super Cocktail Bar with open log fire and over 100 brands of whisky to tempt you. The attractive and comfortable bistro has an extensive and varied menu. An ideal centre for touring, sailing and walking.

Tel: 01631 710483 • Fax: 01631 710694
e-mail: enquiries@fallsoflora.com • www.fallsoflora.com

A warm welcome awaits you in this delightful bungalow set in 20 acres of farmland where we breed our own Highland cattle which graze at the front. It is a peaceful location as we are set back from the road, and an ideal spot for touring, with the main ferry terminal at Oban just 10 minutes away.

Our luxurious rooms have their own special sitting room attached where you can enjoy your coffee or a glass of wine in peace, and we also have our own restaurant where you can dine.

Mrs J. Currie, Hawthorn, 5 Keil Crofts, Benderloch, Oban PA37 1QS

01631 720452

e-mail: june@hawthorncottages.com

www.hawthorncottages.com

The Lancaster

A small family-run, sea front hotel with 27 bedrooms, most of which are en suite, some with sea views. All public rooms enjoy sea views.

Indoor heated swimming pool, steam room, sauna and spa.

There is private parking to the front and rear of the hotel

We are a pet-friendly Hotel. As well as your room, dogs are allowed into all public rooms in the hotel except the dining room

An ideal location from which to explore the Highlands and Islands.

email: lancasteroban@btconnect.com

www.lancasteroban.co.uk • 01631 562587

Esplanade Oban PA34 5AD

Argyll & Bute is a wonderfully unspoilt area, historically the birthplace of Scotland and home to a wealth of fascinating wildlife. Here you may be lucky enough to catch a glimpse of an eagle, a wildcat or an osprey, whales, dolphin, seals, or even a giant octopus. At every step the sea fringed landscape is steeped in history, from prehistoric sculpture at Kilmartin and Knapdale, standing stone circles and Bronze Age cup-and-ring engravings, to the elegant ducal home of the once feared Clan Campbell. On the upper reaches of Loch Caolisport can be found St Columba's Cave, and more recent times are illustrated at the Auchindrain Highland Township south of Inveraray, a friendly little town with plenty to see, including the Jail, Wildlife Park and Maritime Museum.

Ayrshire & Arran

A warm welcome awaits you at our family farm situated in the beautiful Doon Valley. An ideal base for touring Ayrshire or Galloway on the Galloway Tourist Route (A713), 6 miles south of Ayr.

Our spacious farmhouse offers en suite twin/double and family rooms with king size beds and all facilities, lounge, dining room and large garden. We serve a delicious varied farmhouse breakfast, with homebaking and farm produce in season. Enjoy a bedtime tea/coffee or hot chocolate with a home baked cookie. Prestwick Airport guests welcome (whatever the time!). Children and pets welcome. B&B from £22.50 pppn, children half price.

Smithston Farm, Patna, By Ayr KA6 7EZ
Mrs Joyce Bothwell - 01292 531211
e-mail: bothwellfarming@mail.com
www.smithstonfarmhouse.co.uk

Comfortable friendly accommodation is offered on this 200 acre dairy farm well situated for the A736 Glasgow to Irvine road and for the A737; well placed to visit golf courses, country parks, or leisure centre, also ideal for the ferry to Arran or Millport and for many good shopping centres all around.

A high standard of cleanliness is assured by Mrs Gillan who is a first class cook holding many awards, food being served in the diningroom with its beautiful picture windows.

Three comfortable bedrooms (double en suite, family and twin), all with tea-making facilities, central heating and electric blankets. Two bathrooms with shower; sittingroom with colour TV. Children welcome.

Bed and Breakfast from £18 double room; en suite from £23. Dinner can be arranged.

Mrs Jane Gillan, Shotts Farm, Beith KA15 1LB
Tel & Fax: 01505 502273 • e-mail: shotts.farm@btinternet.com

SB

e-mail: eglintonguesthouse@yahoo.co.uk
www.eglintonguesthouse.com

Situated within a part of Ayr steeped in history, within a few minutes' walk of the beach, town centre and many other amenities and entertainment for which Ayr is popular. There are sea and fishing trips available from Ayr Harbour, or a cruise "Doon the Water" on the "Waverley"; golf, swimming pool, cycling, tennis, sailing, windsurfing, walking, etc all available nearby; Prestwick Airport only three miles away.

We have family, double and single rooms, all with washbasins, colour TV and tea/coffee making facilities. En suite facilities and cots available on request. We are open all year round.

Bed and Breakfast from £25. Please send for our brochure for further information.

Peter & Julia Clark, Eglinton Guest House, 23 Eglinton Terrace, Ayr KA7 1JJ • Tel/Fax: 01292 264623

SB

The Ormidale

is a lively pub with seven bedrooms, famous for its home cooked bar meals, real ale and weekend discos. Set in 7 acres of wooded grounds, 5 minutes from beach and shops.

Wi-Fi

• 15 minutes from the ferry terminal
• Magnificent views to Goat Fell
• All bedrooms en suite with colour TV, tea/coffee
• Outstanding bar lunches & suppers • Children's menu
• Fully licensed • CAMRA recommended • Beer garden
• Large car park • Children's play area

Room rate from £40 per person per night bed and full Scottish breakfast.

Ormidale is centrally situated on the island and is convenient for mountain access. Pony trekking, putting, swimming, tennis, bowling and golf (Arran has 7 courses) are other activities easily accessible from the Ormidale.

The pub attracts all ages to the regular weekend discos and midweek quiz nights.

Resident Proprietors: Tommy & Barbara Gilmore
Ormidale Hotel, Brodick, Isle of Arran KA27 8BY
e-mail: reception@ormidale-hotel.co.uk
www.ormidale-hotel.co.uk • Tel: 01770 302293

Brodick

Kilmarnock

West Tannacrieff

Fenwick, Kilmarnock KA3 6AZ

Tel: 01560 600258

mobile: 07773 226332

Fax: 01560 600914

Mrs Nancy Cuthbertson

Wi-Fi

A warm welcome awaits all our guests to our dairy farm, situated in the peaceful Ayrshire countryside. Relax in spacious, well-furnished, en suite rooms with all modern amenities, colour TV and tea/coffee making facilities. Large parking area and garden.

Situated off the M/A77 on the B751 road to Kilmaurs, so easily accessible from Glasgow, Prestwick Airport, and the south. An ideal base for exploring Ayrshire's many tourist attractions.

Enjoy a hearty breakfast with home-made breads and preserves, and home baking for supper. Children welcome. Terms from £30 per person. Brochure available.

e-mail: westtannacrieff@btopenworld.com

www.smoothhound.co.uk/hotels/westtannacrieff.html

Borders

Crossed by the River Tweed, which provides some of the best fishing in Scotland, the
Scottish Borders stretch from the rolling hills and moorland in the west, through gentler
valleys and agricultural plains, to the rocky Berwickshire coastline with its secluded coves
and picturesque fishing villages. This variety of landscape has led to numerous
opportunities for walking, horse riding and cycling, fishing and golf, as well as surfing,
diving and birdwatching on the coast. Friendly towns, long known for their textiles, and
charming villages are there to be discovered, while castles, abbeys, stately homes and
museums illustrate the exciting and often bloody history of the area, commemorated in
the Common Ridings and other local festivals which create a colourful pageant much
enjoyed by visitors and native Borderers alike.

SB

Wi-Fi

Over Langshaw Farm B&B

AA ★★★ Farmhouse

In the beautiful Border hills, near Melrose and Galashiels and only 45 minutes from Edinburgh, is the perfect relaxing place to stay. The farm is run organically and has black and white cows for their creamy milk, brown hens for their delicious eggs, and woolly sheep for their delightful lambs. Lots of home produce, real ice creams and sorbets, breakfast from the red Aga, and all the comforts of a lovely old farmhouse. There is one ground floor double room and one family room (with bathrooms and ever changing views over the valley). Scottish castles and keeps, wildlife areas, walking, riding, mountain biking, fishing, golf, antique shops, eating out and pubs etc are all within easy reach. *B&B from £32.50pppn. Contact Sheila and Martyn Bergius.*

**Over Langshaw Farm, Galashiels,
Scottish Borders TD1 2PE
Tel: 01896 860244
overlangshaw@btconnect.com
www.overlangshawfarm.co.uk**

Wi-Fi

Hundalee House
Jedburgh TD8 6PA
Tel & Fax: 01835 863011

Large historic Manor House set in 15 acres of secluded gardens and woodland near Jedburgh, decorated in a charming Victorian style.

All rooms are en suite, two with four-poster, and all with the expected luxuries including TV, tea/coffee making facilities, hairdryer, central heating, free wireless internet. Children welcome.

*Bed and Breakfast from £28-£33 per person per night.
Single £30-£45.
Reductions for children.*

**e-mail: sheila.whittaker@btinternet.com
www.accommodation-scotland.org**

Melrose, Peebles

Traditional Georgian house, set well away from the road in its own spacious grounds • Peaceful and relaxing atmosphere • Good touring base • A warm welcome awaits you, in a comfortable country house with lovely views

- Accommodation consists of one single room and two twin rooms
- Lift to local pub for supper to accommodate walkers
- Quiet peaceful location with ample parking
- *Terms from: £40 single, £30pp in twin room.*

Contact: Mrs Lee, Mainhill House, St Boswells, Melrose, Roxburghshire TD6 0HG0
Tel: 01835 823788
e-mail: annmainhill@hotmail.co.uk

SB

Clint Lodge
Country Guest House

St Boswells, Melrose TD6 0DZ
Tel: 01835 822027 • Fax: 01835 822656

Enjoy a warm welcome and excellent Bed & Breakfast at this traditional Scottish guest house. The bright and spacious drawing room has an open log fire; small adjoining sun lounge. Residents can enjoy a meal in the atmospheric dining room or a stroll in the large garden. Traditional features have been enhanced, with the old wooden and tiled floors, original fireplaces and wood surrounds adding to Clint Lodge's appealing and relaxing atmosphere.
There are five bedrooms - four are en suite, one of the twin rooms has a private bathroom. All have twin or super king size double beds, tea and coffee making facilities, TV, wifi access.

www.clintlodge.co.uk • e-mail: clintlodge@aol.com   *Ideally located in the heart of the Scottish Borders*

SB

South Mains Farm
is a working family farm, situated in an elevated position with good views, on the B7016 between Biggar and Broughton. An ideal place to take a break on a North/South journey. Edinburgh 29 miles, Peebles 11 miles. Well situated for touring the Border regions in general.

A comfortable bed and excellent breakfast provided in this centrally heated farmhouse. The lounge has a log fire and the bedrooms, two double and one single, have hand-basins, electric blankets and tea/coffee making facilities. Guest bathroom. Open all year. Car essential, parking.

Terms from £24 pppn.
If you are interested just ring,
write or call in.
Warm welcome assured.

Mrs Rosemary Harper,
South Mains Farm,
Biggar ML12 6HF
Tel: 01899 860226

West Linton

SB

&

Wi-Fi

Drochil Castle B&B

Family-run Drochil Castle is a traditional Scottish farmhouse offering a relaxed, friendly welcome. In summer sit and enjoy the view over the garden with its handsome mature trees.
If the weather is less kind unwind by the fireside and enjoy a cup of tea and some home-baking.
Drochil is ideally placed for touring the scenic and historic Scottish border country with its delightful towns, especially Peebles, Melrose and Kelso.
The house is traditionally decorated, very comfortable, warm and welcoming. Every attempt has been made to anticipate your needs. All the bedrooms have tea and coffee making facilities, TV, radio alarm and electric blankets. All linen and towels are provided. Public rooms have comfy sofas and in cooler weather a roaring fire entices guests into the sitting room. Breakfast is served in the conservatory with its spectacular panoramic view.

Ann Black • Drochil Castle B&B
Drochil Castle Farm, Romanno Bridge
Peebles EH46 7DD
Tel: 01721 752249
e-mail: annblack@drochilcastle.co.uk
www.drochilcastle.co.uk

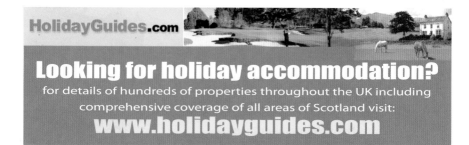

Castle Douglas

Dumfries & Galloway

Warmed by the influence of the Gulf Stream, touring in this quiet corner of south west Scotland is a pleasure, visiting the dozens of interesting castles, gardens, museums and historic sites. In addition a never-ending succession of music festivals, ceilidhs, village fairs, country dances, classical music concerts and children's entertainment guarantees plenty of scope for enjoyment, and for those whose interest is in the night skies a visit to the Galloway Forest Park, the UK's first designated Dark Sky Park, is a 'must'. Discover the many hidden secrets of this lovely and unspoilt landscape such as the pretty little villages along the coast, including the 'Artists' Town', Kirkcudbright, while those who love 'the written word' must surely visit the book town of Wigtown.

symbols 🏇 SB & ♀ Wi-Fi

🐕	Pets Welcome	🏇	Children Welcome
SB	Short Breaks	♿	Suitable for Disabled Guests
♀	Licensed	Wi-Fi	Wi-Fi available

Bathgate, Edinburgh

Edinburgh & Lothians

Wi-Fi

This 17th century farmhouse is situated two miles from M8 Junction 4, which is midway between Glasgow and Edinburgh. This peaceful location overlooks panoramic views of the countryside. All rooms are on the ground floor, ideal for disabled visitors, and have central heating, colour TV and tea/coffee making facilities. We are within easy reach of golf, fishing, cycling (15-mile cycle track runs along back of property). New railway station within 5 minute walk. Edinburgh – Glasgow line.

Scottish TOURIST BOARD ★★★ B&B

Ample security parking.
Open January to December.
Children and pets by arrangement

Twin Room from £44-£55,
Family Room £60-£80

Mrs F. Gibb, Tarrareoch Farm, Station Road, Armadale, Near Bathgate EH48 3BJ
Tel: 01501 730404
tarrareochfarmhouse@talktalk.net

SB

&

Wi-Fi

INTERNATIONAL GUEST HOUSE • EDINBURGH

Conveniently situated 1½ miles south of Princes Street on the main A701, on the main bus route. Private parking. All bedrooms en suite, with direct-dial telephone, colour TV and tea/coffee making facilities. Some rooms enjoy magnificent views across to the extinct volcano of Arthur's Seat. The full Scottish breakfasts served on the finest bone china are a delight.

B&B from £45 to £85 single; £70 to £150 double.

AA ★★★★ Guest House

37 Mayfield Gardens, Edinburgh EH9 2BX
Tel: 0131 667 2511 • Fax: 0131 667 1112
e-mail: intergh1@yahoo.co.uk • www.accommodation-edinburgh.com

CENTRAL EDINBURGH Bed and Breakfast accommodation in the capital of Scotland close to the Kings Theatre and Edinburgh Castle. Our location is in the West End of the city and not far from the busy and famous shopping centre of Princes Street, probably the premier shopping street in Scotland. Close at hand are numerous good restaurants, theatres and the Usher Hall, the main concert hall in the city. Only a five-minute walk from here is the Edinburgh International Conference Centre which is located in the main financial district of the city.

A full Scottish or Continental breakfast awaits you, served with a warm welcome. We are pleased to arrange day tours to Loch Ness and Loch Lomond with a pick-up from the guest house.

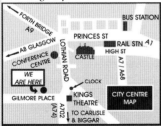

This historic listed building was built in 1750 and to the rear of the house is a beautiful garden, well stocked with herbs and fruit trees. The house is good example of a Georgian town house villa, fully restored but still retaining its original character and style.

City Centre Accommodation with Car Park

SB

CASTLE PARK GUEST HOUSE
75 Gilmore Place, Edinburgh EH3 9NU • Tel: 0131 229 1215 • e-mail: castlepark@btconnect.com

A warm and friendly welcome awaits you at Castle Park Guest House, a charming Victorian Guest House ideally situated close to King's Theatre and city centre. Travel along the Royal Mile with Edinburgh Castle at one end and the Palace of Holyrood House, the Official Scottish Residence of the Queen, at the other end.

Centrally heated throughout, colour TV in all rooms, en suite facilities available, tea/coffee hospitality tray, full Scottish/Continental breakfast. Children welcome – special prices. Car parking available.

www.castleparkguesthouse.co.uk

KENVIE GUEST HOUSE 16 Kilmaurs Road, Edinburgh EH16 5DA

A charming and comfortable Victorian town house situated in a quiet and pleasant residential part of the city, approximately one mile south of the centre and one small block from Main Road (A7) leading to the City and Bypass to all routes. Excellent bus service.

We offer for your comfort, complimentary tea/coffee, central heating, colour TV and No Smoking rooms. En suite rooms available. Lovely breakfasts and lots of additional caring touches.

A warm and friendly welcome is guaranteed from Richard and Dorothy.

Tel: 0131-668 1964 • Fax: 0131-668 1926 • e-mail: dorothy@kenvie.co.uk

SB

Wi-Fi

A large Victorian villa with modern spacious accommodation overlooking historic Linlithgow Palace - centrally located for easy access to all local amenities.

With the Town Centre only a few minutes' walk away the house is within easy reach of the Canal Basin, the main bus and rail terminals, and the motorway network to Glasgow, Edinburgh and Stirling.

Open all year. Credit Cards accepted. B&B available from £40 per night.

STRAWBERRY BANK HOUSE
13 Avon Place, Strawberry Bank, Linlithgow EH49 6BL
Tel & Fax: 01506 848 372   *Mr & Mrs J Caddle*
e-mail: gillian@strawberrybank-scotland.co.uk
www.strawberrybank-scotland.co.uk

ASHCROFT FARMHOUSE
A WARM WELCOME

East Calder, Livingston EH53 0ET
Tel: 01506 881810
ashcroftinfo@aol.com

Award-winning Ashcroft Farmhouse is in the country yet is only 10 miles from Edinburgh City Centre. Six golf-themed en suite bedrooms on ground floor, all with flat-screen digital TV with Freeview. Lovely lounge, fabulous breakfasts and beautiful gardens. Complimentary wi-fi access. No children under 12 years.   **www.ashcroftfarmhouse.co.uk**

Glasgow & District

Kilsyth

Allanfauld Farm

Scottish TOURIST BOARD ★★★ FARMHOUSE

Libby MacGregor, Allanfauld Farm, Kilsyth, Glasgow G65 9DF
Tel & Fax: 01236 822155
e-mail: allanfauld@hotmail.com
www.allanfauld.com

Allanfauld Bed and Breakfast is open all year round. Enjoy a warm Scottish welcome and true farmhouse hospitality at our family home, where we have farmed for almost 100 years.
The working farm sits at the foot of the Kilsyth Hills, a great base to explore central Scotland.

Wi-Fi

Twin/triple/family room • Single room
Both rooms have TV and tea/coffee making facilities.
Visitors have access to a TV and lounge room and Wi-Fi connection.

Both Glasgow and Stirling are a 20 minute drive away. A short train journey will take you into the centre of Glasgow, Edinburgh or Stirling.

There is local access to a wide range of activities and facilities such as a swimming pool, a rock-climbing hotspot, golf courses, hill-walking, fishing and many other tourist attractions.

B&B from £25-£35

Log cabins now available
£70 for 2 people sharing or £450 per week.

The Lodge
available as self-catering or with breakfast served in farmhouse.
Sleeps 2/4.

In one of Europe's most dynamic cultural centres, there's so much to see and do – from the City of Glasgow itself, alive with heritage, architecture, entertainment and nightlife, to the charm of the bustling towns, scenic villages and countryside of the surrounding districts. James Watt, Adam Smith, Charles Rennie Mackintosh, Lord Kelvin and a host of others have all played a major part in Greater Glasgow's past. Today the area has a wealth of attractions which recall their works. Entertainment and sport feature in an exciting year round calendar that encompasses opera and theatre, music of all kinds, Scottish ceilidhs and top sporting events. One of the UK's top shopping centres, Glasgow is home to a multitude of shops, from boutiques and specialist stores, to the High Street favourites, and shopping malls. Out in the easily accessible countryside, follow the famous River Clyde from New Lanark, the site of the historic 18th century mills established by Robert Owen.

Highlands

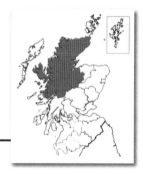

GLENURQUHART *House* HOTEL

Peaceful Tranquillity

Drumnadrochit - Loch Ness - Glen Affric

Escape to the Scottish Highlands

for peace and tranquillity and stay in our comfortable and friendly STB 4 Star Restaurant with Rooms. With fantastic views of Loch Meikle and Glen Urquhart, the house nestles in six acres of wooded grounds close to Loch Ness and Glen Affric nature reserve.

All bedrooms are en suite and have tea/coffee making facilities, hairdryer, colour TV/DVD and bathrobes.

There is a cosy lounge bar warmed by a log fire and an award-winning restaurant serving freshly cooked meals.

We are ideally situated for exploring the Highlands of Scotland; day trips might include visits to the Isle of Skye, a trip to the Highland capital of Inverness or a boat trip to spot dolphins on the Moray Firth.

View of Loch Meikle from the Hotel

GLENURQUHART HOUSE HOTEL

Balnain, Drumnadrochit IV63 6TJ

Carol and Ewan Macleod • Tel: 01456 476234

info@glenurquhart-house-hotel.co.uk • www.glenurquhart-house-hotel.co.uk

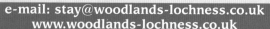

Apart from the stunning and varied scenery, the major attraction of The Scottish Highlands is that there is so much to see and do, whatever the season. Stretching from Fort William in the south, to Wick in the far north, and with access links radiating out from the busy city of Inverness, there is a wealth of visitor attractions and facilities. Perhaps the most famous is Loch Ness, home of the legendary monster, and a good starting point for a sail down the Caledonian Canal, through the unspoiled scenery of the Great Glen to Fort William. Just to the south lies Ben Nevis, Glencoe and a whole range of outdoor sporting activities from fishing and sailing to skiing. In the Cairngorm National Park it's possible to glimpse an osprey or capercaillie while walking, climbing, skiing or cycling, or just enjoying the stunning mountain scenery.

Glencoe

Kingussie

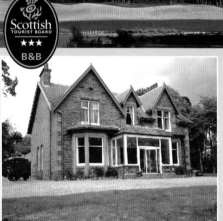

Thurso, Whitebridge

This former 19th century coaching inn on the John O'Groats peninsula is set in six acres of parkland, close to the Queen Mother's former Highland home, the Castle of Mey.

Fully modernised, the hotel has eight centrally heated en suite bedrooms with colour television and tea making facilities; the spacious Pentland Suite offers a double and family room with en suite bathroom.

Locally caught salmon, crab and other fine Highland produce feature on the varied table d'hôte and grill menus available in the Garden Room, while lighter meals and snacks can be enjoyed in the cosy Pentland Lounge.

A warm Highland welcome awaits you.

**www.castlearms.co.uk
Tel & Fax: 01847 851244
e-mail: castlearms.mey@btinternet.com**

symbols

🐕	Pets Welcome	🎠	Children Welcome
SB	Short Breaks	♿	Suitable for Disabled Guests
♉	Licensed	Wi-Fi	Wi-Fi available

Lanarkshire

SB

A modern farmhouse bungalow on Dykecroft Farm, set in lovely surroundings in a rural area on the B7086 (old A726) and within easy reach of the M74, making it the ideal stop between north and south; also convenient for Glasgow and Prestwick airports. Centrally situated for touring Glasgow, Edinburgh, Ayr, Stirling and New Lanark - all within one hour's drive. Nearby is Strathclyde Country Park with all watersports activities; other sporting facilities within two miles include sports centre, golf, fishing, quad bikes, rifle and clay pigeon shooting, and swimming. Guests will enjoy the open fires in our TV lounge and the good breakfasts; TV and tea making facilities in all rooms. A warm and friendly welcome awaits all guests.

Dykecroft Farm

Scottish
TOURIST BOARD
★★
B&B

Boghead, Kirkmuirhill,
Lesmahagow ML11 0JQ
e-mail: Dykecroft.bandb@tiscali.co.uk

Tel & Fax: 01555 892226
www.Dykecroftfarm.co.uk

Perth & Kinross

SB

Wi-Fi

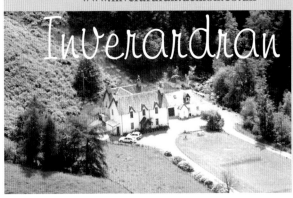

Stanley

Newmill Farm

Stanley PH1 4QD
Mrs Ann Guthrie •01738 828281
e-mail: guthrienewmill@sol.co.uk
www.newmillfarm.co.uk

This 330-acre farm is situated on the A9, six miles north of Perth.
Accommodation comprises twin and double en suite rooms and a family room with private bathroom;
lounge, sittingroom, diningroom; bathroom, shower room and toilet.
The warm welcome and supper of excellent home baking are inclusive. Reductions and facilities
for children. Pets accepted. Ample car parking area. Excellent local restaurants nearby.
The numerous castles and historic ruins around Perth are testimony to Scotland's turbulent past. Situated in

the area known as "The Gateway to the Highlands" the farm is
ideally placed for those seeking some of the best unspoilt scenery in
Western Europe. Many famous golf courses and trout rivers in the
Perth. If walking or cycling are your interests, there are plenty of
routes around the farm that are worth exploring to enjoy the views.

Double/Twin from £32pppn
Single from £45 per night

Stirling
& The Trossachs

A walk through the medieval Old Town of Stirling, one of Scotland's newest cities, is the ideal starting point for touring the area, then explore the wild glens and sparkling lochs in Loch Lomond and The Trossachs National Park, and perhaps take a steamer trip down Loch Katrine. Whatever your fitness, there are walks suitable for everyone, cycle routes, challenging mountain bike trails, golf and wildlife. The amazing Falkirk Wheel linking the Forth and Clyde and Union Canals is a sight and experience not to be missed, while villages and small towns such as Drymen, Killearn, Fintry and Kippen offer hospitality and interesting outings less than an hour from Glasgow, yet feels worlds apart from the bustle of city life.

Broadford

Scottish Islands

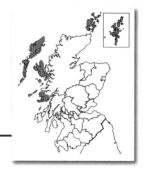

Hillview is a large house with stunning views over Broadford Bay towards Torridon and Applecross.
The B&B has a double bedroom with en suite facilities, a double bedroom with shared facilities, and a twin room with shared facilities, as well as a family room with a private bathroom and a balcony. We offer a full Scottish breakfast or vegetarian option if you prefer. Our rooms are very comfortable and most have stunning sea views.

Hillview B&B is an ideal base for exploring surrounding area. The scenery is wild and dramatic, with the Cuillin range being the island's most famous feature. The landscape varies from the strange rock formations of the Quirang to the lushness of the Garden of Skye in the south of the island. Around Broadford there are numerous mountain and coastal walks for all abilities.

Isabel MacLeod, Hillview, Blackpark, Broadford, Isle of Skye IV49 9DE
e-mail: isabel@hillview-skye.co.uk • Telephone: 01471 822 083
www.hillview-skye.co.uk

So many islands are waiting to be visited off the Scottish mainland, each with a mystery and magic of its own. To the north lie the Orkney and Shetland Isles, with their strong connections to the Vikings whose influence is still seen and heard today. To the west, exposed to the Atlantic, lie the Inner and Outer Hebrides, including the islands of Skye, Islay, Mull and Tiree, Lewis, Harris and Barra, each with its own culture, traditions and heritage. Everywhere there's evidence of settlement going back to prehistoric times, including awe-inspiring standing stones and circles and chambered cairns. Some islands have mountains to climb, but most are low-lying, ideal for exploring on foot and for cycling and bird watching, while the Atlantic waves have proved a great attraction to surfers from all over the world.!.

Kirkwall

Brae

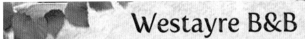

Pubs & Inns

A selection of inns, pubs and hostelries offering food, refreshment and traditional good cheer; many also provide comfortable overnight accommodation.

🛏 Accommodation available

🍽 Food available

🅿 Parking

 Wi-Fi available

🐎 Pets welcome

🐎 Children welcome

This 16th century Inn with its low beamed ceiling boasts a suntrap courtyard garden during the summer and a roaring log fire during the winter months, giving it a wonderful traditional ambience. There's always a selection of real ales and lagers on offer in the bar which is open from morning 'til night, every day. The inn has five comfortable and very well appointed en suite guest bedrooms. An ideal base for exploring this scenic area.

Black Cock Inn, Princes Street, Broughton-in-Furness, Cumbria LA20 6HQ

Tel: 01229 716529
www.blackcockinncumbria.com
e-mail: theblackcockinn20@gmail.com

The Plough
AT EATON

**Macclesfield Road, Eaton,
Near Congleton, Cheshire CW12 2NH
Tel: 01260 280207 • Fax: 01260 298458**

Traditional oak beams and blazing log fires in winter reflect the warm and friendly atmosphere of this half-timbered former coaching inn which dates from the 17th century.

The heart of the 'Plough' is the kitchen where food skilfully prepared is calculated to satisfy the most discerning palate. Luncheons and dinners are served seven days a week with traditional roasts on Sundays.

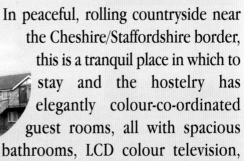

In peaceful, rolling countryside near the Cheshire/Staffordshire border, this is a tranquil place in which to stay and the hostelry has elegantly colour-co-ordinated guest rooms, all with spacious bathrooms, LCD colour television, direct-dial telephone and tea and coffee-making facilities amongst their impressive appointments. Wireless internet access available.

**e-mail: theploughinn@hotmail.co.uk
www.theploughinnateaton.co.uk**

Horse & Farrier Inn

Threlkeld • Keswick • Cumbria

For over 300 years The Horse & Farrier has enjoyed an idyllic location in the centre of the picturesque village of Threlkeld, just 4 miles east of Keswick. Situated beneath Blencathra, with stunning views looking over towards the Helvellyn Range, this traditional Lakeland Inn offers a warm Cumbrian welcome to all its customers.

Mellow Lakeland stone, traditional architecture and such a peaceful setting make the Horse & Farrier a perfect place to enjoy a quiet pint, delicious food or a short break "away from it all". With superb Lakeland walks on your doorstep including Blencathra and Skiddaw and the Cumbria Way, we're ideally situated for walkers.

Our Restaurant is well known locally for the quality and imagination of its food and our Bar serves some of the best Jennings real ales in the Lake District.

Together with our 9 well appointed en suite bed & breakfast rooms, this really is a special place to spend some time. Well behaved pets are welcome.

Horse & Farrier Inn, Threlkeld, Keswick, Cumbria CA12 4SQ
Tel: 017687 79688 • Fax: 017687 79823
info@horseandfarrier.com • www.horseandfarrier.com

★★★★ INN

Pet-Friendly Accommodation

A selection of properties where pets are welcome.
Please contact individual proprietors for full details
and whether there is any charge for pets.

Counties are arranged in A-Z order within each country.

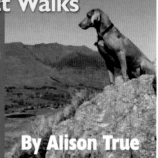
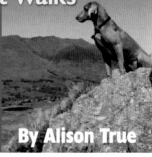

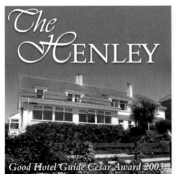

Visit the FHG website
www.holidayguides.com
for all kinds of holiday accommodation in Britain

DIRECTORY OF WEBSITE AND E-MAIL ADDRESSES

A quick-reference guide to holiday accommodation with an e-mail address and/or website, conveniently arranged by country and county, with full contact details.

•LONDON

Hotel
Athena Hotel, 110-114 Sussex Gardens, Hyde Park, LONDON W2 1UA
Tel: 020 7706 3866
• e-mail: stay@athenahotellondon.co.uk
• website: www.athenahotel.co.uk

•BERKSHIRE

Touring Campsite
Wellington Country Park, Odiham Road, Riseley, Near READING, Berkshire RG7 1SP
Tel : 0118 932 6444
• e-mail: info@wellington-country-park.co.uk
• website: www.wellington-country-park.co.uk

•CHESHIRE

Farmhouse B & B
Astle Farm East, Chelford, MACCLESFIELD, Cheshire SK10 4TA
Tel: 01625 861270
• e-mail: stubg@aol.com
• website: www.astlefarmeast.co.uk

•CORNWALL

Self-Catering
Penrose Burden Holiday Cottages, St Breward, BODMIN, Cornwall PL30 4LZ
Tel : 01208 850277
• website: www.penroseburden.co.uk

Self-Catering / Caravan
Mrs A. E. Moore, Hollyvagg Farm, Lewannick, LAUNCESTON, Cornwall PL15 7QH
Tel: 01566 782309
• website: www.hollyvaggfarm.co.uk

Self- Catering
Mr Lowman, Cutkive Wood Holiday Lodges, St Ive, LISKEARD, Cornwall PL14 3ND
Tel: 01579 362216
• e-mail: holidays@cutkivewood.co.uk
• website: www.cutkivewood.co.uk

Self-Catering
Butterdon Mill Holiday Homes, Merrymeet, LISKEARD, Cornwall PL14 3LS
Tel: 01579 342636
• e-mail: butterdonmill@btconnect.com
• website: www.bmhh.co.uk

Caravan / Camping
Quarryfield Caravan & Camping Park, Crantock, NEWQUAY, Cornwall
Contact: Mrs A Winn, Tretherras, Newquay, Cornwall TR7 2RE
Tel: 01637 872792
• e-mails: quarryfield@crantockcaravans.orangehome.co.uk info@quarryfield.co.uk
• website: www.quarryfield.co.uk

B&B
Bolankan Cottage B & B, Crows-an-Wra, St Buryan, PENZANCE, Cornwall TR19 6HU
Tel: 01736 810168
• e-mail: bolankancottage@talktalk.net
• website: www.bolankan-cottage.co.uk

Caravan / Camping
Globe Vale Holiday Park, Radnor, REDRUTH, Cornwall TR16 4BH
Tel: 01209 891183
• e-mail: info@globevale.co.uk
• website: www.globevale.co.uk

Guest House
Mr S Hope, Dalswinton House, ST MAWGAN-IN-PYDAR, Cornwall TR8 4EZ
Tel: 01637 860385
• e-mail: dalswintonhouse@btconnect.com
• website: www.dalswinton.com

Self-Catering
Maymear Cottage, ST TUDY
Contact: Ruth Reeves, Polstraul, Trewalder,
Delabole, Cornwall PL33 9ET
Tel: 01840 213120
• e-mail: ruth.reeves@hotmail.co.uk
• website: www.maymear.co.uk

Self-Catering
The Garden House, Port Isaac, Near
WADEBRIDGE, Cornwall
Contact: Mr D Oldham, Trevella,
Treveighan, St Teath, Cornwall PL30 3JN
Tel: 01208 850529
• e-mail: david.trevella@btconnect.com
• website: www.trevellacornwall.co.uk

•CUMBRIA

Caravan Park
Greenhowe Caravan Park, Great Langdale,
AMBLESIDE, Cumbria LA22 9JU
Tel: 015394 37231
•e-mail: enquiries@greenhowe.com
•website: www.greenhowe.com

B&B
Smallwood House, Compston Road,
AMBLESIDE, Cumbria LA22 9DH
Tel: 015394 32330
• website: www.smallwoodhotel.co.uk

Self-Catering
Mrs Almond, Irton House Farm, Isel, Near
KESWICK, Cumbria CA13 9ST
Tel: 017687 76380
• e-mail: joan@irtonhousefarm.co.uk
• website: www.irtonhousefarm.com

Self-Catering
Mr D Williamson, Derwent Water Marina,
Portinscale, KESWICK, Cumbria CA12 5RF
Tel: 017687 72912
• e-mail: info@derwentwatermarina.co.uk
• website: www.derwentwatermarina.co.uk

Self-Catering
Mrs S.J. Bottom, Crossfield Cottages,
KIRKOSWALD, Penrith, Cumbria CA10 1EU
Tel: 01768 898711
• e-mail: info@crossfieldcottages.co.uk
• website: www.crossfieldcottages.co.uk

•DERBYSHIRE

Self-Catering Holiday Cottages
Mark Redfern, Paddock House Farm Holiday
Cottages, Peak District National Park,
Alstonefield, ASHBOURNE, Derbyshire
DE6 2FT
Tel: 01335 310282 / 07977 569618
• e-mail: info@paddockhousefarm.co.uk
• website: www.paddockhousefarm.co.uk

Caravan
Golden Valley Caravan Park, Coach Road,
RIPLEY, Derbyshire DE55 4ES
Tel: 01773 513881
• e-mail:
enquiries@goldenvalleycaravanpark.co.uk
• website: www.goldenvalleycaravanpark.co.uk

•DEVON

Self-Catering
Mrs A. Bell, Wooder Manor, Widercombe-in-
the-Moor, Near ASHBURTON, Devon
TQ13 7TR
Tel: 01364 621391
• website: www.woodermanor.com

Hotel
Fairwater Head Hotel, Hawkchurch, Near
AXMINSTER, Devon EX13 5TX
Tel: 01297 678349
• e-mail: stay@fairwaterheadhotel.co.uk
• website: www.fairwaterheadhotel.co.uk

Self-Catering / B&B
Lake House Cottages and B&B, Lake
Villa, BRADWORTHY, Devon EX22 7SQ
Tel : 01409 241962
• email: lesley@lakevilla.co.uk
• website: www.lakevilla.co.uk

Self-Catering
Linda & Jim Watt, Northcote Manor
Farm Holiday Cottages, Kentisbury,
COMBE MARTIN, Devon EX31 4NB
Tel: 01271 882376
• e-mail: info@northcotemanorfarm.co.uk
• website: www.northcotemanorfarm.co.uk

Self-Catering
G Davidson Richmond, Clooneavin,
Clooneavin Path, LYNMOUTH, Devon
EX35 6EE
Tel: 01598 753334
• e-mail: relax@clooneavinholidays.co.uk
• website: www.clooneavinholidays.co.uk

FHG Guides

Guest House
Mr. & Mrs D. Fitzgerald, Beaumont, Castle Hill, SEATON, Devon EX12 2QW
Tel: 01297 20832
- e-mail: beaumont.seaton@talktalk.net
- website:
www.smoothhound.co.uk/hotels/beaumon1.html

Caravans / Camping
Salcombe Regis Camping & Caravan Park, SIDMOUTH, Devon EX10 0JH
Tel: 01395 514303
- e-mail: contact@salcombe-regis.co.uk
- website: www.salcombe-regis.co.uk

Self-Catering / Camping
Dartmoor Country Holidays, Magpie Leisure Park, Bedford Bridge, Horrabridge, Yelverton, TAVISTOCK, Devon PL20 7RY
Tel: 01822 852651
- website: www.dartmoorcountryholidays.co.uk

Caravan & Camping
North Morte Farm Caravan & Camping Park, Mortehoe, WOOLACOMBE, Devon EX34 7EG
Tel: 01271 870381
- e-mail: info@northmortefarm.co.uk
- website: www.northmortefarm.co.uk

•DORSET

Self-Catering
C. Hammond, Stourcliffe Court, 56 Stourcliffe Avenue, Southbourne, BOURNEMOUTH, Dorset BH6 3PX
Tel: 01202 420698
- e-mail: rjhammond1@hotmail.co.uk
- website: www.stourcliffecourt.co.uk

Self-Catering Cottage / Farmhouse B & B
Mrs S. E. Norman, Frogmore Farm, Chideock, BRIDPORT, Dorset DT6 6HT
Tel: 01308 456159
- e-mail: bookings@frogmorefarm.com
- website: www.frogmorefarm.com

B&B
Nethercroft, Winterbourne Abbas, DORCHESTER, Dorset DT2 9LU
Tel: 01305 889337
- e-mail: val.bradbeer@btconnect.com
- website: www.nethercroft.com

Farmhouse B&B / Caravan & Camping
Luckford Wood Farmhouse, Church Street, East Stoke, Wareham, Near LULWORTH, Dorset BH20 6AW
Tel: 01929 463098 / 07888 719002
- e-mail: luckfordleisure@hotmail.co.uk
- website: www.luckfordleisure.co.uk

Self-Catering
Westover Farm Cottages, Wootton Fitzpaine, Near LYME REGIS, Dorset DT6 6NE
Tel: 01297 560451/07979 265064
- e-mail: wfcottages@aol.com
- website: www.westoverfarmcottages.co.uk

Hotel
The Knoll House, STUDLAND BAY, Dorset BH19 3AH
Tel: 01929 450450
- e-mail: info@knollhouse.co.uk
- website: www.knollhouse.co.uk

Inn B&B
The White Swan, The Square, 31 High Street, SWANAGE BN19 2LJ
Tel: 01929 423804
- e-mail: info@whiteswanswanage.co.uk
- website: www.whiteswanswanage.co.uk

•GLOUCESTERSHIRE

Self-Catering
Two Springbank, 37 Hopton Road, Cam, DURSLEY, Gloucs GL11 5PD
Contact: Mrs F A Jones, 32 Everlands, Cam, Dursley, Gloucs G11 5NL
Tel: 01453 543047
- e-mail: info@twospringbank.co.uk
- website: www.twospringbank.co.uk

B & B
Mrs A Rhoton, Hyde Crest, Cirencester Road, Minchinhampton, STROUD, Gloucs GL6 8PE
Tel: 01453 731631
- e-mail: stay@hydecrest.co.uk
- website: www.hydecrest.co.uk

•HAMPSHIRE

Holiday Park
Downton Holiday Park, Shorefield Road, Milford-on-Sea, LYMINGTON, Hampshire SO41 0LH
Tel: 01425 476131 / 01590 642515
- e-mail: info@downtonholidaypark.co.uk
- website: www.downtonholidaypark.co.uk

•LANCASHIRE

Guest House
Parr Hall Farm, Parr Lane, Eccleston, Chorley, PRESTON, Lancs PR7 5SL
Tel: 01257 451917
- e-mail: enquiries@parrhallfarm.com
- website: www.parrhallfarm.com

•NORFOLK

Self-catering
Scarning Dale, Dale Road, Scarning,
DEREHAM, Norfolk NR19 2QN
Tel: 01362 687269
• e-mail: jean@scarningdale.co.uk
• website: www.scarningdale.co.uk

Holiday Park
Waveney Valley Holiday Park, Airstation
Lane, Rushall, DISS, Norfolk IP21 4QF
Tel: 01379 741228
• e-mail: waveneyvalleyhp@aol.com
• website: www.caravanparksnorfolk.co.uk

Self-Catering
Blue Riband Holidays, HEMSBY,
Great Yarmouth, Norfolk NR29 4HA
Tel: 01493 730445
• websites: www.blueribandrolidays.co.uk
www.parklandshemsby.co.uk

Self-Catering
Winterton Valley Holidays, Edward Road,
WINTERTON-ON-SEA, Norfolk NR29 4BX
Contact:15 Kingston Avenue, Caister-on-
Sea, Norfolk NR30 5ET
Tel: 01493 377175
• e-mail: info@wintertonvalleyholidays.co.uk
• website: www.wintertonvalleyholidays.co.uk

•NOTTINGHAMSHIRE

Caravan & Camping Park
Orchard Park, Marnham Road, Tuxford,
NEWARK, Nottinghamshire NG22 0PY
Tel: 01777 870228
• e-mail: info@orchardcaravanpark.co.uk
• website: www.orchardcaravanpark.co.uk

•OXFORDSHIRE

B&B
Middle Fell, Moreton Road, Aston Upthorpe,
DIDCOT, Oxfordshire OX11 9ER
Tel: 01235 850207
• e-mail: middlefell@ic24.net
• website: www.middlefell.co.uk

B & B / Guest House
June Collier, Colliers B&B, 55 Nethercote
Road, Tackley, KIDLINGTON, Oxfordshire
OX5 3AT
Tel: 01869 331255 / 07790 338225
• e-mail: junecollier@btinternet.com
• website: www.colliersbnb.co.uk

•SHROPSHIRE

Self-Catering
Clive & Cynthia Prior, Mocktree Barns
Holiday Cottages, Leintwardine, LUDLOW,
Shropshire SY7 0LY
Tel: 01547 540441
• e-mail: mocktreebarns@care4free.net
• website: www.mocktreeholidays.co.uk

Self-Catering
Jane Cronin, Sutton Court Farm Cottages,
Sutton Court Farm, Little Sutton, LUDLOW,
Shropshire SY8 2AJ
Tel: 01584 861305
• e-mail: enquiries@suttoncourtfarm.co.uk
• website: www.suttoncourtfarm.co.uk

•SOMERSET

Farm / Guest House / Self-Catering
Jackie Bishop, Toghill House Farm, Freezing
Hill, Wick, Near BATH, Somerset BS30 5RT
Tel: 01225 891261
• e-mail:
accommodation@toghillhousefarm.co.uk
• website: www.toghillhousefarm.co.uk

Self-Catering
Westward Rise Holiday Park, South Road,
BREAN, Burnham-on-Sea, Somerset TA8 2RD
Tel: 01278 751310
• e-mail: info@westwardrise.com
• website: www.westwardrise.com

Self-Catering / Holiday Park / Touring Pitches
James Randle, St Audries Bay Holiday Club,
West Quantoxhead, MINEHEAD, Somerset
TA4 4DY
Tel: 01984 632515
• e-mail: info@staudriesbay.co.uk
• website: www.staudriesbay.co.uk

Farm / Guest House
G. Clark, Yew Tree Farm, THEALE,
Near Wedmore, Somerset BS28 4SN
Tel: 01934 712475
• e-mail: enquiries@yewtreefarmbandb.co.uk
• website: www.yewtreefarmbandb.co.uk

•SUFFOLK

Self-Catering
Kessingland Cottages, Rider Haggard Lane,
KESSINGLAND, Suffolk.
Contact: S. Mahmood, 156 Bromley Road,
Beckenham, Kent BR3 6PG
Tel: 020 8650 0539
• e-mail: jeeptrek@kjti.co.uk
• website: www.k-cottage.co.uk

Holiday Park
Broadland Holiday Village, Oulton
Broad, LOWESTOFT, Suffolk NR33 9JY
Tel: 01502 573033
• e-mail: info@broadlandvillage.co.uk
• website: www.broadlandvillage.co.uk

•EAST SUSSEX

Hotel
Grand Hotel, 1 Grand Parade, St Leonards,
HASTINGS, East Sussex TN37 6AQ
Tel: 01424 428510
• e-mail: info@grandhotelhastings.co.uk
• website: www.grandhotelhastings.co.uk

Self-Catering
"Pekes", CHIDDINGLY, East Sussex
Contact: Eva Morris, 124 Elm Park
Mansions, Park Walk, London SW10 0AR
Tel: 020 7352 8088
• e-mail: pekes.afa@virgin.net
• website: www.pekesmanor.com

Guest House / Self-Catering
Longleys Farm Cottage, Harebeating Lane,
HAILSHAM, East Sussex BN27 1ER
Tel: 01323 841227
• website: www.longleysfarmcottage.co.uk

• WEST SUSSEX

Guest Accommodation
St Andrews Lodge, Chichester Road,
SELSEY, West Sussex PO20 0LX
Tel: 01243 606899
• e-mail: info@standrewslodge.co.uk
• website: www.standrewslodge.co.uk

•WARWICKSHIRE

Guest House
John & Julia Downie, Holly Tree
Cottage, Pathlow, STRATFORD-UPON-
AVON, Warwickshire CV37 0ES
Tel: 01789 204461
• e-mail: john@hollytree-cottage.co.uk
• website: www.hollytree-cottage.co.uk

•NORTH YORKSHIRE

Self-Catering
Rudding Holiday Park, Follifoot,
HARROGATE, North Yorkshire HG3 1JH
Tel: 01423 870439
• e-mail: stay@ruddingpark.com
• website: www.ruddingholidaypark.co.uk

Self-Catering
Southfield Farm Holiday Cottages,
Darley, HARROGATE, North Yorkshire
HG3 2PR
Tel: 01423 780258
• e-mail: info@southfieldcottages.co.uk
• website: www.southfieldcottages.co.uk

Farmhouse B & B
Mrs Julie Clarke, Middle Farm, Woodale,
Coverdale, LEYBURN, North Yorkshire
DL8 4TY
Tel: 01969 640271
• e-mail: j-a-clarke@hotmail.co.uk
• www.yorkshirenet.co.uk/stayat/middlefarm/
index.htm

Self-Catering
2 Hollies Cottages, Stainforth, SETTLE,
N.Yorkshire
Contact : Bridge Cottage, Stainforth,
Near Settle BD24 9PG
Tel: 01729 822649
• e-mail: vivmills30@hotmail.com
• website: www.stainforth-holiday-cottage-
settle.co.uk

Self-Catering
York Lakeside Lodges Ltd, Moor Lane,
YORK, North Yorkshire YO24 2QU
Tel: 01904 702346
• e-mail: neil@yorklakesidelodges.co.uk
• website: www.yorklakesidelodges.co.uk

Bestselling holiday accommodation guides for over 65 years

WALES

•ANGLESEY & GWYNEDD

Self-Catering Chalet
Chalet at Glan Gwna Holiday Park, Caethro,
CAERNARFON, Gwynedd
Contact: Mr H A Jones, 12 Lon Isaf, Menai
Bridge, Anglesey LL59 5LN
Tel: 01248 712045
• e-mail: hajones@northwales-chalet.co.uk
• website: www.northwales-chalet.co.uk

Self-Catering
Parc Wernol, Chwilog Fawr, Chwilog,
PWLLHELI, Criccieth, Gwynedd LL53 6SW
Tel: 01766 810506
• e-mail: catherine@wernol.co.uk
• website: www.wernol.co.uk

• PEMBROKESHIRE

Self-Catering
Llanteglos Estate, Llanteg, Near
AMROTH, Pembs SA67 8PU
• e-mail: llanteglosestate@supanet.com
• website: www.llanteglos-estate.com

Self-Catering
Timberhill Farm, BROAD HAVEN,
Pembrokeshire SA62 3LZ
Contact: Mrs L Ashton, 10 St Leonards
Road, Thames Ditton, Surrey KT7 0RJ
Tel: 02083 986349
• e-mail: lejash@aol.com
• website: www.33timberhill.co

Self-Catering
Quality Cottages, Cerbid, Solva,
HAVERFORDWEST, Pembrokeshire SA62 6YE
Tel: 01348 837871
• e-mail: reserve@qualitycottages.co.uk
• website: www.qualitycottages.co.uk

Self-Catering
Ffynnon Ddofn, Llanon, Llanrhian, Near ST
DAVIDS, Pembrokeshire.
Contact: Mrs B. Rees White, Brick House
Farm, Burnham Road, Woodham Mortimer,
Maldon, Essex CM9 6SR. Tel: 01245 224611
• e-mail: daisypops@madasafish.com
• website: www.ffynnonddofn.co.uk

•POWYS

Self-Catering
Lane Farm, Paincastle, BUILTH WELLS,
Powys LD2 3JS
Tel: 01497 851 605
• e-mail: lanefarm@onetel.com
• website: www.lane-farm.co.uk

SCOTLAND

•ARGYLL & BUTE

Self-Catering
Appin House Lodges, APPIN, Argyll
PA38 4BN
Tel: 01631 730207
• e-mail: denys@appinhouse.co.uk
• website: www.appinhouse.co.uk

Self-Catering
Blarghour Farm Cottages, Blarghour Farm,
By Dalmally, INVERARAY, Argyll PA33 1BW
Tel: 01866 833246
• e-mail: blarghour@btconnect.com
• website: www.self-catering-argyll.co.uk

Hotel
Falls of Lora Hotel, Connel Ferry, By OBAN,
Argyll PA37 1PB
Tel: 01631 710483
• e-mail: enquiries@fallsoflora.com
• website: www.fallsoflora.com

•DUMFRIES & GALLOWAY

Hotel
Corsewall Lighthouse Hotel, Kirkcolm,
STRANRAER, Dumfries & Galloway
DG9 0QG Tel: 01776 853220
• e-mail info@lighthousehotel.co.uk
• website: www.lighthousehotel.co.uk

•EDINBURGH & LOTHIANS

Self-Catering
Mrs C. M. Kilpatrick, Slipperfield House,
WEST LINTON, Peeblesshire EH46 7AA
Tel: 01968 660401
• e-mail: cottages@slipperfield.com
• website: www.slipperfield.com

•HIGHLANDS

Self-Catering
Frank & Juliet Spencer-Nairn, Culligran
Cottages, Struy, Near BEAULY, Inverness-
shire IV4 7JX . Tel: 01463 761285
• e-mail: info@culligrancottages.co.uk
• website: www.culligrancottages.co.uk

FHG Guides

Caravan Park
A.J.Davis, Gruinard Bay Caravan Park,
LAIDE, Ross-shire IV22 2ND
Tel: 01445 731225
• **e-mail: gruinard@ecosse.net**
• **website: www.gruinardbay.co.uk**

•PERTH & KINROSS

Self-Catering
Atholl Cottage, Killiecrankie, PITLOCHRY,
Perthshire PH16 5LR
Contact: Mrs Joan Troup, Dalnasgadh,
Killiecrankie, Pitlochry, Perthshire PH16 5LN
Tel: 01796 470017
• **e-mail: info@athollcottage.co.uk**
• **website: www.athollcottage.co.uk**

•ORKNEY

Caravan & Camping
Point of Ness, STROMNESS, Orkney
Tel: 01856 873535
• **e-mail: leisureculture@orkney.gov.uk**
• **websites: www.orkney.gov.uk**
   www.hostelsorkney.co.uk

NORTHERN IRELAND

Caravan Park
Six Mile Water Carvan Park, Lough
Road, ANTRIM BT41 4DG
Tel: 028 9446 4963
• **e-mail: sixmilewater@antrim.gov.uk**
• **website: www.antrim.gov.uk/caravanpark**

INTERNET & Wi-Fi Access

•OXFORDSHIRE

DIDCOT • *B&B*

Middle Fell B&B, Moreton Road, Aston Upthorpe, Didcot OX11 9ER
Tel: 01235 850207 or 07833 920678
e-mail: middlefell@ic24.net
website: www.middlefell.co.uk
Wi-Fi connection in every room free of charge.

Accommodation Standards: Star Grading Scheme

The AA, VisitBritain, VisitScotland, and the VisitWales now use a single method of assessing and rating serviced accommodation. Irrespective of which organisation inspects an establishment the rating awarded will be the same, using a common set of standards, giving a clear guide of what to expect. They have full details of the grading system on their websites.

   www.visitScotland.com

 www.visitWales.com   www.theaa.com

Using a scale of 1-5 stars the objective quality ratings give a clear indication of accommodation standard, cleanliness, ambience, hospitality, service and food.

The more stars, the higher level of quality

This shows the full range of standards suitable for every budget and preference, and allows visitors to distinguish between the quality of accommodation and facilities on offer in different establishments.

All types of board and self-catering accommodation are covered, including hotels, B&Bs, holiday parks, campus accommodation, hostels, caravans and camping, and boats.

Gold and Silver awards are given to Hotels and Guest Accommodation that provide exceptional quality, especially in service and hospitality.

★
acceptable quality; simple, practical, no frills

★★
good quality, well presented and well run

★★★
very good level of quality and comfort

★★★★
excellent standard throughout

★★★★★
exceptional quality, with a degree of luxury

National Accessible Scheme Logos for mobility impaired and older people

If you have particular mobility impairment. look out for the National Accessible Scheme. You can be confident of finding accommodation or attractions that meet your needs by looking for the following symbols.

 Older and less mobile guests
If you have sufficient mobility to climb a flight of steps but would benefit from fixtures and fittings to aid balance.

 Part-time wheelchair users
You have restricted walking ability or may need to use a wheelchair some of the time and can negotiate a maximum of 3 steps.

 Independent wheelchair users
You are a wheelchair user and travel independently. Similar to the international logo for independent wheelchair users.

 Assisted wheelchair users
You're a wheelchair user and travel with a friend or family member who helps you with everyday tasks.

READERS' OFFER 2013

BEKONSCOT MODEL VILLAGE & RAILWAY
Warwick Road, Beaconsfield,
Buckinghamshire HP9 2PL
Tel: 01494 672919
e-mail: info@bekonscot.co.uk
www.bekonscot.co.uk

*One child FREE when accompanied by two
full-paying adults. Valid February to October 2013*

NOT TO BE USED IN CONJUNCTION WITH ANY OTHER OFFER

READERS' OFFER 2013

NENE VALLEY RAILWAY
Wansford Station, Stibbington,
Peterborough, Cambs PE8 6LR
Tel: 01780 784444
e-mail: nvrorg@nvr.org.uk
www.nvr.org.uk

One child FREE with each full paying adult.
Valid Jan. to end Oct. 2013 (excludes galas and pre-ticketed events)

NOT TO BE USED IN CONJUNCTION WITH ANY OTHER OFFER

READERS' OFFER 2013

TAMAR VALLEY DONKEY PARK
St Ann's Chapel, Gunnislake,
Cornwall PL18 9HW
Tel: 01822 834072
e-mail: info@donkeypark.com
www.donkeypark.com

*£1 OFF per person, up to 6 persons
Valid from Easter until end October 2013*

NOT TO BE USED IN CONJUNCTION WITH ANY OTHER OFFER

READERS' OFFER 2013

LAPPA VALLEY RAILWAY
Benny Halt, St Newlyn East,
Newquay, Cornwall TR8 5LX
Tel: 0844 4535543
e-mail: info@lappavalley.co.uk
www.lappavalley.co.uk

*£1 per person OFF up to a maximum of £4. Valid Easter
to end October 2013 (not on Family Saver tickets)*

NOT TO BE USED IN CONJUNCTION WITH ANY OTHER OFFER

Be a giant in a magical miniature world of make-believe depicting rural England in the 1930s. "A little piece of history that is forever England."

Open: 10am-5pm daily mid February to end October.

Directions: Junction 16 M25, Junction 2 M40.

FHG GUIDES, ABBEY MILL BUSINESS CENTRE, PAISLEY PA1 1TJ • www.holidayguides.com

---

Take a trip back in time on the delightful Nene Valley Railway with its heritage steam and diesel locomotives, There is a 7½ mile ride from Wansford to Peterborough via Yarwell, with shop, museum and excellent cafe at Wansford Station (free parking).

Open: please phone or see website for details.

Directions: situated 4 miles north of Peterborough on the A1

FHG GUIDES, ABBEY MILL BUSINESS CENTRE, PAISLEY PA1 1TJ • www.holidayguides.com

---

Cornwall's only Donkey Sanctuary set in 14 acres overlooking the beautiful Tamar Valley. Donkey grooming, goat hill, children's playgrounds, cafe and picnic area. All-weather play barn. Well behaved dogs on leads welcome.

Open: Easter to end Oct: daily 10am to 5pm. Nov to March: weekends and all school holidays 10.30am to 4.30pm

Directions: just off A390 between Callington and Gunnislake at St Ann's Chapel.

FHG GUIDES, ABBEY MILL BUSINESS CENTRE, PAISLEY PA1 1TJ • www.holidayguides.com

---

Three miniature railways, plus leisure park with canoes, crazy golf, large children's play area with fort, brickpath maze, wooded walks (all inclusive). Dogs welcome (50p).

Open: Easter to end October

Directions: follow brown tourist signs from A30 and A3075

FHG GUIDES, ABBEY MILL BUSINESS CENTRE, PAISLEY PA1 1TJ • www.holidayguides.com

**READERS'
OFFER
2013**

THE BEACON
West Strand, Whitehaven,
Cumbria CA28 7LY
Tel: 01946 592302 • Fax: 01946 598150
e-mail: thebeacon@copelandbc.gov.uk
www.thebeacon-whitehaven.co.uk

One FREE adult/concesssion when accompanied by one full paying
adult/concession. Under 16s free. Valid from Oct 2012 to end 2013.
Not valid for special events. Day tickets only.

NOT TO BE USED IN CONJUNCTION WITH ANY OTHER OFFER

**READERS'
OFFER
2013**

DEVONSHIRE COLLECTION OF PERIOD COSTUME
Totnes Fashion & Textiles Museum,
Bogan House, 43 High Street,
Totnes, Devon TQ9 5NP
Tel: 01803 862857 • www.devonmuseums.net

FREE child with a paying adult with voucher
Valid from Spring Bank Holiday to end of Sept 2013

NOT TO BE USED IN CONJUNCTION WITH ANY OTHER OFFER

**READERS'
OFFER
2013**

WOODLANDS FAMILY THEME PARK
Blackawton, Dartmouth,
Devon TQ9 7DQ
Tel: 01803 712598 • Fax: 01803 712680
e-mail: fun@woodlandspark.com
www.woodlandspark.com

15% discount off full individual admission price.
No photocopies. Valid 30 March to 1st November 2013.

NOT TO BE USED IN CONJUNCTION WITH ANY OTHER OFFER

**READERS'
OFFER
2013**

THE MILKY WAY ADVENTURE PARK
The Milky Way, Clovelly,
Bideford, Devon EX39 5RY
Tel: 01237 431255
e-mail: info@themilkyway.co.uk
www.themilkyway.co.uk

10% discount on entrance charge.
Valid Easter to end October (not August).

NOT TO BE USED IN CONJUNCTION WITH ANY OTHER OFFER

The Beacon is the Copeland area's interactive museum, tracing the area's rich history, from as far back as prehistoric times to the modern day. Enjoy panoramic views of the Georgian town and harbour from the 4th floor viewing gallery. Art gallery, gift shop, restaurant. Fully accessible.

Open: open all year (excl. 24-26 Dec) Tues-Sun, plus Monday Bank Holidays. Please contact before visit to check.

Directions: enter Whitehaven from north or south on A595. Follow the town centre and brown museum signs; located on harbourside.

FHG GUIDES, ABBEY MILL BUSINESS CENTRE, PAISLEY PA1 1TJ • www.holidayguides.com

---

Themed exhibition, changed annually, based in a Tudor house. Collection contains items of dress for women, men and children from 17th century to 1990s, from high fashion to everyday wear.

Open: Open from 22 May to end September. 11am to 5pm Tuesday to Friday.

Directions: centre of town, opposite Market Square. Mini bus up High Street stops outside.

FHG GUIDES, ABBEY MILL BUSINESS CENTRE, PAISLEY PA1 1TJ • www.holidayguides.com

---

A wide variety of rides, plus zoo and farm, makes a fantastic day out for all ages. Awesome indoor adventure centres, ball blasting arenas, mirror maze and soft play ensures wet days are fun. 16 family rides including white knuckle Swing Ship, electrifying Watercoasters, terrifying Toboggan Run, Superb Falconry Centre, Zoo Farm, tractor ride, weird and wonderful creatures. An all-weather attraction.

Open: 23 March to 3 November 2013 open daily 9.30am. In winter open weekends and local school holidays.

Directions: 5 miles from Dartmouth on A3122. Follow brown tourist signs from A38.

FHG GUIDES, ABBEY MILL BUSINESS CENTRE, PAISLEY PA1 1TJ • www.holidayguides.com

---

The day in the country that's out of this world! With 5 major rides and loads of great live shows. See Merlin from 'Britain's Got Talent' 5 days a week. All rides and shows included in entrance fee.

Open: daily Easter to October. Please call or check online for full details.

Directions: on the main A39 one mile from Clovelly.

FHG GUIDES, ABBEY MILL BUSINESS CENTRE, PAISLEY PA1 1TJ • www.holidayguides.com

Entertainment for all ages: fascinating daily shows, FREE wagon and tractor rides, straw fun barn, go-kart arena, gypsy wagons and Romany talks, blacksmith's workshop. Drive a real tractor, pony rides, 'hands-on' activities with the farm animals, over 20 rescued heavy horses. Lots undercover; cafe and gift shop + much more!

Open: 10am to 5pm Easter to end October.

Directions: On the Edmondsham Road, approx. 1½ miles from Verwood. Within easy reach of Bournemouth, Poole, Southampton, Ringwood and surrounding areas.

FHG GUIDES, ABBEY MILL BUSINESS CENTRE, PAISLEY PA1 1TJ • www.holidayguides.com

Killhope is a multi-award winning Victorian Lead Mining Museum, offering a grand day out. Accompany a guide on a mine tour. Our enthusiastic team ensure you have a day to remember, finding minerals, and working as a washerboy. Woodland trails, exhibitions, Killhope shop and cafe complete a great day out.

Open: April-October 10.30am-5pm

Directions: midway between Alston and Stanhope on A689

FHG GUIDES, ABBEY MILL BUSINESS CENTRE, PAISLEY PA1 1TJ • www.holidayguides.com

Children's farm and petting centre. Lots of hands on with bottle feeding events and bunny cuddling etc. Indoor and outdoor play areas, indoor and outdoor go-kart tracks, crazy golf, gift shop, tea room and lots more.

Open: March to Oct: 10am-5pm daily; Nov to Feb 10am to 4pm daily. Closed Christmas, Boxing Day and New Year's Day.

Directions: A181 from A19, head towards coast; signposted from there.

FHG GUIDES, ABBEY MILL BUSINESS CENTRE, PAISLEY PA1 1TJ • www.holidayguides.com

Set in over 700 acres of unspoilt Essex countryside, this former working farm is one of the county's most popular tourist attractions. The spectacular craft village and educational farm provide the perfect setting for a great day out.

Open: 7 days a week. March to October 10am-5pm; November to February 10am-4pm.

Directions: follow brown tourist signs from A127 and A12.

FHG GUIDES, ABBEY MILL BUSINESS CENTRE, PAISLEY PA1 1TJ • www.holidayguides.com

FHG

·K·U·P·E·R·A·R·D·

READERS' OFFER 2013

CIDER MUSEUM & KING OFFA DISTILLERY
21 Ryelands Street, Hereford,
Herefordshire HR4 0LW
Tel: 01432 354207
e-mail: enquiries@cidermuseum.co.uk
www.cidermuseum.co.uk

TWO for the price of ONE admission
Valid to end December 2013

NOT TO BE USED IN CONJUNCTION WITH ANY OTHER OFFER

FHG

·K·U·P·E·R·A·R·D·

READERS' OFFER 2013

SHEPRETH WILDLIFE PARK
Station Road, Shepreth,
Near Royston, Herts SG8 6PZ
Tel: 01763 262226
e-mail: office@sheprethwildlifepark.co.uk
www.sheprethwildlifepark.co.uk

FREE child with paying adult. Valid until 31/12/013
(excluding weekends and school holidays).

NOT TO BE USED IN CONJUNCTION WITH ANY OTHER OFFER

FHG

·K·U·P·E·R·A·R·D·

READERS' OFFER 2013

THE HELICOPTER MUSEUM
The Heliport, Locking Moor Road,
Weston-Super-Mare BS24 8PP
Tel: 01934 635227
e-mail: helimuseum@btconnect.com
www.helicoptermuseum.co.uk

One child FREE with two full-paying adults
Valid from April to December 2013

NOT TO BE USED IN CONJUNCTION WITH ANY OTHER OFFER

FHG

·K·U·P·E·R·A·R·D·

READERS' OFFER 2013

WEDGWOOD VISITOR CENTRE
Wedgwood Drive, Barlaston,
Stoke-on-Trent, Staffordshire ST12 9ER
Tel: 01782 282986 • Fax: 01782 223063
e-mail: bookings@wwrd.com
www.wedgwoodvisitorcentre.com

W
WEDGWOOD
Visitor Centre

TWO for ONE offer on admission to Visitor Centre
(cheapest ticket free). Valid until end December 2013

NOT TO BE USED IN CONJUNCTION WITH ANY OTHER OFFER

Learn how traditional cider and perry was made, how the fruit was harvested, milled, pressed and bottled. Walk through original champagne cider cellars, and view 18th century lead crystal cider glasses.

Open:
April to Oct: 10am-5pm Mon-Sat.
Nov to March: 11am-3pm Mon-Sat.

Directions: off A438 Hereford to Brecon road, near Sainsbury's supermarket.

Wildlife park with a variety of species including tigers, mountain lions, meerkats, monkeys and otters. Indoor attractions include Waterworld, Bug City and Ringo's Playbarn.

Open: daily 10am-6pm (until dusk Winter/Spring). November-February closed Tuesday and Wednesday.

Directions: signposted off A10 between Royston and Cambridge. Two minutes from Shepreth rail station on Cambridge - London Kings X line.

The world's largest helicopter collection - over 70 exhibits, includes two royal helicopters, Russian Gunship and Vietnam veterans plus many award-winning exhibits. Cafe, shop. Flights.

PETS MUST BE KEPT UNDER CONTROL

Open: Wednesday to Sunday 10am to 5.30pm. Daily during school Easter and Summer holidays and Bank Holiday Mondays. November to March: 10am to 4.30pm

Directions: Junction 21 off M5 then follow the propellor signs.

The Wedgwood Factory, Visitor Centre and Museum is set in 260 acres of lush parkland. Enjoy a fascinating tour of the ceramic workshops and museum, guided factory tours, and the opportunity to make your own piece of Wedgwood at the home of Britain's greatest ceramic company.

Open: weekdays 10am-5pm weekends 10am-4pm

Directions: from M1 follow A50 west; from M6 follow A34, then brown tourist signs.

FALCONRY UK BIRDS OF PREY CENTRE

Sion Hill Hall, Kirby Wiske
Near Thirsk, North Yorkshire YO7 4EU
Tel: 01845 587522
e-mail: mail@falconrycentre.co.uk
www.falconrycentre.co.uk

READERS' OFFER 2013

TWO for ONE on admission to Centre. Cheapest ticket free with voucher. Valid 1st March to 31st October.

NOT TO BE USED IN CONJUNCTION WITH ANY OTHER OFFER

MUSEUM OF RAIL TRAVEL

Ingrow Railway Centre, Near Keighley,
West Yorkshire BD21 5AX
Tel: 01535 680425
e-mail: admin@vintagecarriagestrust.org
www.vintagecarriagestrust.org

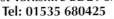

READERS' OFFER 2013

"ONE for ONE" free admission
Valid during 2013 except during special events (ring to check)

NOT TO BE USED IN CONJUNCTION WITH ANY OTHER OFFER

RHEILFFORDD TALYLLYN RAILWAY

Gorsaf Wharf Station, Tywyn,
Gwynedd LL36 9EY
Tel: 01654 710472
e-mail: enquiries@talyllyn.co.uk
www.talyllyn.co.uk

READERS' OFFER 2013

20% OFF ticket price of full adult round trip
Not valid on special/excursion trains or Christmas services

NOT TO BE USED IN CONJUNCTION WITH ANY OTHER OFFER

INIGO JONES SLATEWORKS

Groeslon, Caernarfon,
Gwynedd LL54 7UE
Tel: 01286 830242
e-mail: slate@inigojones.co.uk
www.inigojones.co.uk

READERS' OFFER 2013

TWO for the price of ONE on self-guided tour.
Valid during 2013

NOT TO BE USED IN CONJUNCTION WITH ANY OTHER OFFER

Birds of prey centre with over 70 birds including owls, hawks, falcons, kites, vultures and eagles. 3 flying displays daily. When possible public welcome to handle birds after each display. No dogs allowed.

Open: 1st March to 31st October 10.30am to 5pm. Flying displays 11.30am, 1.30pm and 3.30pm daily (weather permitting).

Directions: on the A167 between Northallerton and the Ripon turn off. Follow brown tourist signs.

FHG GUIDES, ABBEY MILL BUSINESS CENTRE, PAISLEY PA1 1TJ • www.holidayguides.com

---

A fascinating display of railway carriages and a wide range of railway items telling the story of rail travel over the years.

ALL PETS MUST BE KEPT ON LEADS

Open: daily 11am to 4pm

Directions: approximately one mile from Keighley on A629 Halifax road. Follow brown tourist signs

FHG GUIDES, ABBEY MILL BUSINESS CENTRE, PAISLEY PA1 1TJ • www.holidayguides.com

---

The Talyllyn Railway is a historic narrow-gauge steam railway running through the beautiful mid-Wales countryside, from Tywyn on the coast to the delightful Dolgoch Falls and wooded Nant Gwernol.

Open: daily from Easter to October and at other times of the year. See website for details of timetables.

Directions: on the A493 on the Aberdyfi side of Tywyn, 300 yards from Tywyn mainline rail station and bus stops.

FHG GUIDES, ABBEY MILL BUSINESS CENTRE, PAISLEY PA1 1TJ • www.holidayguides.com

---

A unique, thriving, fully operational slateworks. Enter the workshops for a fascinating and inspiring insight into an ongoing era of techniques and expertise. Self-guided tours including Lettercutting and Calligraphy Exhibitions.

Open: seven days a week 9am-5pm. Closed Christmas/Boxing/New Year's days

Directions: main A487 6 miles south of Caernarfon going towards Porthmadog.

FHG GUIDES, ABBEY MILL BUSINESS CENTRE, PAISLEY PA1 1TJ • www.holidayguides.com

GWILI RAILWAY
The Railway Station,
Bronwydd Arms,
Carmarthenshire SA33 6HT
Tel: 01267 238213
www.gwili-railway.co.uk

READERS' OFFER 2013

TWO FOR ONE (lowest price ticket free). Valid March-Oct 2013 except Thomas or "Special" events and/or Christmas

NOT TO BE USED IN CONJUNCTION WITH ANY OTHER OFFER

THE GRASSIC GIBBON CENTRE
Arbuthnott, Laurencekirk,
Aberdeenshire AB30 1PB
Tel: 01561 361668
e-mail: lgginfo@grassicgibbon.com
www.grassicgibbon.com

READERS' OFFER 2013

TWO for the price of ONE entry to exhibition (based on full adult rate only). Valid during 2013 (not groups)

NOT TO BE USED IN CONJUNCTION WITH ANY OTHER OFFER

BO'NESS & KINNEIL RAILWAY
Bo'ness Station, Union Street,
Bo'ness, West Lothian EH51 9AQ
Tel: 01506 822298
e-mail: enquiries.railway@srps.org.uk
www.bkrailway.com

READERS' OFFER 2013

FREE child train fare with one paying adult/concession. Valid April-Oct 2013. Not Premier Fare events

NOT TO BE USED IN CONJUNCTION WITH ANY OTHER OFFER

SCOTTISH DEER CENTRE
Cupar,
Fife KY15 4NQ
Tel: 01337 810391
e-mail: info@tsdc.co.uk
www.tsdc.co.uk

READERS' OFFER 2013

One child FREE with one full paying adult on production of voucher. Not valid during December.

NOT TO BE USED IN CONJUNCTION WITH ANY OTHER OFFER

During operating days we provide a trip back in time with a round trip on a steam-hauled locomotive in the scenic Gwili valley.
Pay once and ride all day.
Check website or phone for timetables.

Open: check website or phone for information.

Directions: just off the A484, three miles north of Carmarthen.

FHG GUIDES, ABBEY MILL BUSINESS CENTRE, PAISLEY PA1 1TJ • www.holidayguides.com

---

Visitor Centre dedicated to the much-loved Scottish writer Lewis Grassic Gibbon. Exhibition, cafe, gift shop. Outdoor children's play area. Disabled access throughout.

Open: daily March to October 10am to 4.30pm. Groups by appointment including evenings.

Directions: on the B967, accessible and signposted from both A90 and A92.

FHG GUIDES, ABBEY MILL BUSINESS CENTRE, PAISLEY PA1 1TJ • www.holidayguides.com

---

Steam and heritage diesel passenger trains from Bo'ness to Manuel.
Explore the history of Scotland's railways in the Museum of Scottish Railways.
Coffee shop and souvenir shop.

Open: weekends April to October, most days in July and August.
See website for dates and timetables.

Directions: in the town of Bo'ness. Leave M9 at Junction 3 or 5, then follow brown tourist signs.

FHG GUIDES, ABBEY MILL BUSINESS CENTRE, PAISLEY PA1 1TJ • www.holidayguides.com

---

55-acre park with 14 species of deer from around the world.
Guided tours, trailer rides, treetop walkway, children's adventure playground and picnic area.
Other animals include wolves, foxes, otters and a bird of prey centre.

Open: 10am to 5pm daily except Christmas Day and New Year's Day.

Directions: A91 south of Cupar. Take J9 M90 from the north, J8 from the south.

FHG GUIDES, ABBEY MILL BUSINESS CENTRE, PAISLEY PA1 1TJ • www.holidayguides.com

Index of Towns and Counties

Aberdeen, Aberdeen, Banff & Moray	SCOTLAND
Alfriston, East Sussex	SOUTH EAST
Alnmouth, Northumberland	NORTH EAST
Alnmouth, Northumberland	PET-FRIENDLY
Alnwick, Northumberland	NORTH EAST
Alston, Cumbria	NORTH WEST
Ambleside, Cumbria	NORTH WEST
Anglesey, Anglesey & Gwynedd	WALES
Appleby-in-Westmorland, Cumbria	NORTH WEST
Ardfern, Argyll & Bute	SCOTLAND
Arundel, West Sussex	SOUTH EAST
Ashbourne, Derbyshire	EAST MIDLANDS
Ashbourne, Derbyshire	PET-FRIENDLY
Ashbourne, Derbyshire	PUBS & INNS
Ashford, Kent	SOUTH EAST
Aviemore, Highlands	SCOTLAND
Aylesbury, Buckinghamshire	SOUTH EAST
Aylsham, Norfolk	EAST
Ayr, Ayrshire & Arran	SCOTLAND
Ballachulish, Argyll & Bute	SCOTLAND
Balterley, Cheshire	NORTH WEST
Bamburgh, Northumberland	NORTH EAST
Banbury, Oxfordshire	SOUTH EAST
Banchory, Aberdeen, Banff & Moray	SCOTLAND
Bangor, Anglesey & Gwynedd	WALES
Barnstaple, Devon	SOUTH WEST
Barton-on-Sea, Hampshire	SOUTH EAST
Barton-upon-Humber, Lincolnshire	EAST MIDLANDS
Bath, Somerset	SOUTH WEST
Bathgate, Edinburgh & Lothians	SCOTLAND
Beaminster, Dorset	SOUTH WEST
Beamish, Durham	NORTH EAST
Beith, Ayrshire & Arran	SCOTLAND
Belton-in-Rutland, Leicestershire & Rutland	
	EAST MIDLANDS
Berwick-Upon-Tweed, Northumberland	NORTH EAST
Betws-y-Coed, North Wales	WALES
Beverley, East Yorkshire	YORKSHIRE
Bicester, Oxfordshire	SOUTH EAST
Bideford, Devon	SOUTH WEST
Bigbury-on-Sea, Devon	PET-FRIENDLY
Birmingham, West Midlands	HEART OF ENGLAND
Blackpool, Lancashire	NORTH WEST
Bodmin, Cornwall	SOUTH WEST
Bognor Regis, West Sussex	SOUTH EAST
Boscastle, Cornwall	SOUTH WEST
Bournemouth, Dorset	SOUTH WEST
Bowness-on-Windermere, Cumbria	NORTH WEST
Bradford, Scottish Islands/Skye	SCOTLAND
Bradworthy, Devon	SOUTH WEST
Brae, Scottish Islands/Shetland	SCOTLAND
Bridlington, East Yorkshire	YORKSHIRE
Bridport, Dorset	SOUTH WEST
Brighton, East Sussex	SOUTH EAST
Bristol, Somerset	SOUTH WEST
Broadstairs, Kent	SOUTH EAST
Brockenhurst, Hampshire	SOUTH EAST
Brodick, Ayrshire & Arran	SCOTLAND
Broughton-in-Furness, Cumbria	NORTH WEST
Broughton-in-Furness, Cumbria	PUBS & INNS
Bude, Cornwall	SOUTH WEST
Builth Wells, Powys	PET-FRIENDLY
Bunessan, Argyll & Bute	SCOTLAND
Bungay, Suffolk	EAST
Burghill, Herefordshire	HEART OF ENGLAND
Burton Joyce, Nottinghamshire	EAST MIDLANDS
Burwell, Cambridgeshire	EAST
Burwell, Cambridgeshire	PET-FRIENDLY
Buttermere. Cumbria	NORTH WEST
Caldbeck, Cumbria	NORTH WEST
Callander, Stirling & The Trossachs	SCOTLAND
Callington, Cornwall	SOUTH WEST
Cambridge, Camabridgeshire	EAST
Canterbury, Kent	SOUTH EAST
Cardigan, Ceredigion	WALES
Carlisle, Cumbria	NORTH WEST
Carperby, North Yorkshire	YORKSHIRE
Carperby, North Yorkshire	PET-FRIENDLY
Castle Douglas, Dumfries & Galloway	SCOTLAND
Castleton, Derbyshire	EAST MIDLANDS
Chale, Isle of Wight	SOUTH EAST
Cheltenham, Gloucestershire	SOUTH WEST
Chester, Cheshire	NORTH WEST
Chesterfield, Derbyshire	EAST MIDLANDS
Chinley, Derbyshire	EAST MIDLANDS
Chipping Campden, Gloucestershire	SOUTH WEST
Chorley, Lancashire	NORTH WEST
Christleton (Chester), Cheshire	NORTH WEST
Church Stretton, Shropshire	HEART OF ENGLAND
Clare, Suffolk	EAST
Cockermouth, Cumbria	NORTH WEST
Cockermouth, Cumbria	PET-FRIENDLY
Congresbury, Somerset	SOUTH WEST
Coniston, Cumbria	NORTH WEST
Conwy, Anglesey & Gwynedd	WALES
Conwy, North Wales	WALES
Cornhill on Tweed, Borders	SCOTLAND
Corsham, Wiltshire	SOUTH WEST
Cowbridge, South Wales	WALES
Crewe, Cheshire	NORTH WEST
Crianlarich, Perth & Kinross	SCOTLAND
Criccieth, Anglesey & Gwynedd	WALES

Cromer, Norfolk	PET-FRIENDLY
Cullingworth, West Yorkshire	YORKSHIRE
Danby, North Yorkshire	YORKSHIRE
Dartmoor, Devon	SOUTH WEST
Dartmoor, Devon	PET-FRIENDLY
Dartmouth, Devon	SOUTH WEST
Daventry, Northamptonshire	EAST MIDLANDS
Dawlish, Devon	SOUTH WEST
Derby, Derbyshire	EAST MIDLANDS
Devizes, Wiltshire	SOUTH WEST
Didcot, Oxfordshire	SOUTH EAST
Dittisham, Devon	SOUTH WEST
Dolgellau, Anglesey & Gwynedd	WALES
Doncaster, South Yorkshire	YORKSHIRE
Dorchester, Dorset	SOUTH WEST
Droitwich Spa, Worcestershire	HEART OF ENGLAND
Drumnadrochit, Highlands	SCOTLAND
Dulverton, Somerset	SOUTH WEST
Dunoon, Argyll & Bute	SCOTLAND
Dunster, Somerset	SOUTH WEST
Eastbourne, East Sussex	SOUTH EAST
Eaton, Cheshire	PUBS & INNS
Eccleshall, Staffordshire	HEART OF ENGLAND
Eckington, Worcestershire	HEART OF ENGLAND
Edinburgh, Edinburgh & Lothians	SCOTLAND
Elton, Nottinghamshire	EAST MIDLANDS
Exeter, Devon	SOUTH WEST
Exmoor, Devon	SOUTH WEST
Exmoor, Somerset	SOUTH WEST
Exmouth, Devon	SOUTH WEST
Fakenham, Norfolk	EAST
Falmouth, Cornwall	SOUTH WEST
Faversham, Kent	SOUTH EAST
Felixstowe, Suffolk	EAST
Folkestone, Kent	SOUTH EAST
Forres, Aberdeen, Banff & Moray	SCOTLAND
Fort William, Highlands	SCOTLAND
Framlingham, Suffolk	EAST
Freshwater, Isle of Wight	SOUTH EAST
Gainsborough, Lincolnshire	EAST MIDLANDS
Gairloch, Highlands	SCOTLAND
Galashiels, Borders	SCOTLAND
Gatehouse of Fleet, Dumfries & Galloway	SCOTLAND
Gilsland, Cumbria	NORTH WEST
Glaisdale, North Yorkshire	YORKSHIRE
Glastonbury, Somerset	SOUTH WEST
Glencoe, Highlands	SCOTLAND
Glossop, Derbyshire	EAST MIDLANDS
Gloucester, Gloucestershire	SOUTH WEST
Goathland, North Yorkshire	YORKSHIRE
Gomshall, Surrey	PUBS & INNS
Goudhurst, Kent	SOUTH EAST
Gower Peninsula, South Wales	WALES
Great Malvern, Worcestershire	HEART OF ENGLAND
Great Yarmouth, Norfolk	EAST
Gretna Green, Dumfries & Galloway	SCOTLAND
Hailsham, East Sussex	SOUTH EAST
Happisburgh, Norfolk	PET-FRIENDLY
Harrogate, North Yorkshire	YORKSHIRE
Hastings, East Sussex	SOUTH EAST
Haverfordwest, Pembrokeshire	WALES
Hayling Island, Hampshire	SOUTH EAST
Hay-on-Wye, Powys	WALES
Helmsley, North Yorkshire	YORKSHIRE
Henfield, West Sussex	SOUTH EAST
Henley-on-Thames, Oxfordshire	SOUTH EAST
Hexham, Northumberland	NORTH EAST
Holmes Chapel, Cheshire	NORTH WEST
Honiton, Devon	SOUTH WEST
Hook, Hampshire	SOUTH EAST
Horley, Surrey	SOUTH EAST
Horncastle, Lincolnshire	EAST MIDLANDS
Howgill, Cumbria	NORTH WEST
Ilfracombe, Devon	SOUTH WEST
Invergarry, Highlands	SCOTLAND
Inverness, Highlands	SCOTLAND
Isle of Gigha, Argyll & Bute	SCOTLAND
Jedburgh, Borders	SCOTLAND
Jedburgh, Borders	PET-FRIENDLY
Kelso, Borders	SCOTLAND
Kelvedon, Essex	EAST
Kenilworth, Warwickshire	HEART OF ENGLAND
Keswick, Cumbria	NORTH WEST
Keswick, Cumbria	PET-FRIENDLY
Keswick, Cumbria	PUBS & INNS
Kettering, Northamptonshire	EAST MIDLANDS
Kilburn, North Yorkshire	YORKSHIRE
Kilburn, North Yorkshire	PUBS & INNS
Kilmarnock, Ayrshire & Arran	SCOTLAND
Kilsyth, Glasgow & District	SCOTLAND
Kingsbridge, Devon	SOUTH WEST
Kingston upon Thames, Surrey	SOUTH EAST
Kingussie, Highlands	SCOTLAND
Kinlochbervie, Highlands	SCOTLAND

Kirkby Stephen, Cumbria	NORTH WEST
Kirkton, Dumfries & Galloway	SCOTLAND
Kirkwall, Scottish Islands/Orkney	SCOTLAND
Langton-by-Wragby, Lincolnshire	EAST MIDLANDS
Ledbury, Herefordshire	HEART OF ENGLAND
Lesmahagow, Lanarkshire	SCOTLAND
Leyburn, North Yorkshire	YORKSHIRE
Lifton, Devon	SOUTH WEST
Lingfield, Surrey	SOUTH EAST
Linlithgow, Edinburgh & Lothians	SCOTLAND
Liskeard, Cornwall	SOUTH WEST
Livingston, Edinburgh & Lothians	SCOTLAND
Lizard, Cornwall	SOUTH WEST
Llandrindod Wells, Powys	WALES
Llandudno, North Wales	WALES
Lochinver, Highlands	SCOTLAND
London (Central & Greater)	SOUTH EAST
Long Hanborough, Oxfordshire	SOUTH EAST
Long Stratton, Norfolk	EAST
Longframlington, Northumberland	NORTH EAST
Looe, Cornwall	SOUTH WEST
Louth, Lincolnshire	EAST MIDLANDS
Ludlow, Shropshire	HEART OF ENGLAND
Lymington, Hampshire	SOUTH EAST
Lynmouth, Devon	SOUTH WEST
Lynton/Lynmouth, Devon	SOUTH WEST
Macclesfield, Cheshire	NORTH WEST
Maidstone, Kent	SOUTH EAST
Maidstone, Kent	PET-FRIENDLY
Malham, North Yorkshire	YORKSHIRE
Malmesbury, Wiltshire	SOUTH WEST
Malvern Wells, Worcestershire	HEART OF ENGLAND
Mansfield, Nottinghamshire	EAST MIDLANDS
Marlborough, Wiltshire	SOUTH WEST
Maryport, Cumbria	NORTH WEST
Mawgan Porth, Cornwall	SOUTH WEST
Mayfield, Derbyshire	EAST MIDLANDS
Melrose, Borders	SCOTLAND
Melton Mowbray, Leicestershire & Rutland	
	EAST MIDLANDS
Merstham, Surrey	SOUTH EAST
Middleton, Staffordshire	HEART OF ENGLAND
Milford-on-Sea, Hampshire	SOUTH EAST
Minehead, Somerset	SOUTH WEST
Minster Lovell, Oxfordshire	SOUTH EAST
Moffat, Dumfries & Galloway	SCOTLAND
Monmouth, South Wales	WALES
Montgomery, Powys	WALES
Moretonhamstead, Devon	SOUTH WEST
Much Hadham, Hertfordshire	EAST
Nairn, Highlands	SCOTLAND
Nantwich, Cheshire	NORTH WEST
Neath, South Wales	WALES
New Forest, Hampshire	SOUTH EAST
Newby Bridge, Cumbria	NORTH WEST
Newquay, Cornwall	SOUTH WEST
Newtonmore, Highlands	SCOTLAND
Newtonmore, Highlands	PET-FRIENDLY
Northallerton, North Yorkshire	YORKSHIRE
Norwich, Norfolk	EAST
Oban, Argyll & Bute	SCOTLAND
Oban, Argyll & Bute	PET-FRIENDLY
Okehampton, Devon	SOUTH WEST
Ossett, West Yorkshire	YORKSHIRE
Otterburn, Northumberland	NORTH EAST
Ottery St Mary, Devon	SOUTH WEST
Oxford, Oxfordshire	SOUTH EAST
Padstow, Cornwall	SOUTH WEST
Paignton, Devon	SOUTH WEST
Parkend, Gloucestershire	SOUTH WEST
Peebles, Borders	SCOTLAND
Penrith, Cumbria	NORTH WEST
Penzance, Cornwall	SOUTH WEST
Peterborough, Lincolnshire	EAST MIDLANDS
Pickering, North Yorkshire	YORKSHIRE
Plockton, Highlands	SCOTLAND
Plymouth, Devon	SOUTH WEST
Polegate, East Sussex	SOUTH EAST
Polzeath, Cornwall	SOUTH WEST
Porlock, Somerset	SOUTH WEST
Portland, Dorset	SOUTH WEST
Quantock Hills, Somerset	SOUTH WEST
Ravenstonedale, Cumbria	NORTH WEST
Ravenstonedale, Cumbria	PET-FRIENDLY
Reay, Highlands	SCOTLAND
Richmond, North Yorkshire	YORKSHIRE
Rickmansworth, Hertfordshire	EAST
Ripon, North Yorkshire	YORKSHIRE
Ross-on-Wye, Herefordshire	HEART OF ENGLAND
Rothbury, Northumberland	NORTH EAST
Rothesay, Argyll & Bute	SCOTLAND
Ryde, Isle of Wight	SOUTH EAST
St Agnes, Cornwall	SOUTH WEST
St Austell, Cornwall	SOUTH WEST
St Clears, Carmarthenshire	WALES
St Clears, Carmarthenshire	PET-FRIENDLY
St Martins, Perth & Kinross	SCOTLAND
Salisbury, Wiltshire	SOUTH WEST
Saundersfoot, Pembrokeshire	WALES
Saxmundham, Suffolk	EAST
Scarborough, North Yorkshire	YORKSHIRE
Seahouses, Northumberland	NORTH EAST
Seaton, Devon	SOUTH WEST
Selsey, West Sussex	SOUTH EAST
Sheffield, South Yorkshire	YORKSHIRE
Shepton Mallet, Somerset	SOUTH WEST
Sherborne, Dorset	SOUTH WEST
Shillingstone, Dorset	SOUTH WEST
Sidmouth, Devon	SOUTH WEST
Skipton, North Yorkshire	YORKSHIRE

South Molton, Devon	SOUTH WEST
Southampton, Hampshire	SOUTH EAST
Spalding (Lincs), Norfolk	EAST
Spean Bridge, Highlands	SCOTLAND
Stafford, Staffordshire	HEART OF ENGLAND
Staithes, North Yorkshire	YORKSHIRE
Stanley, Perth & Kinross	SCOTLAND
Stow-on-the-Wold, Gloucestershire	SOUTH WEST
Stratford-Upon-Avon, Warwickshire	HEART OF ENGLAND
Strathyre, Stirling & The Trossachs	SCOTLAND
Stroud, Gloucestershire	SOUTH WEST
Sutton-in-Ashfield, Nottinghamshire	EAST MIDLANDS
Swanage, Dorset	SOUTH WEST
Swansea, South Wales	WALES
Tackley/Kidlington, Oxfordshire	SOUTH EAST
Taunton, Somerset	SOUTH WEST
Telford, Shropshire	HEART OF ENGLAND
Tenterden, Kent	SOUTH EAST
Theale, Somerset	SOUTH WEST
Thirsk, North Yorkshire	YORKSHIRE
Thornton-le-Dale, North Yorkshire	YORKSHIRE
Thurso, Highlands	SCOTLAND
Tiverton, Devon	SOUTH WEST
Torquay, Devon	SOUTH WEST
Trearddur Bay, Anglesey & Gwynedd	WALES
Truro, Cornwall	SOUTH WEST
Ullapool, Highlands	SCOTLAND
Ullswater, Cumbria	NORTH WEST
Ulverston, Cumbria	NORTH WEST
Wadebridge, Cornwall	SOUTH WEST
Wareham (nr Lulworth), Dorset	SOUTH WEST
Wells, Somerset	SOUTH WEST
Wells-next-the-Sea, Norfolk	EAST
Welshpool, Powys	WALES
Weobley, Herefordshire	HEART OF ENGLAND
West Linton, Borders	SCOTLAND
Weston-super-Mare, Somerset	SOUTH WEST
Whitby, North Yorkshire	YORKSHIRE
Whitebridge, Highlands	SCOTLAND
Whithorn, Dumfries & Galloway	SCOTLAND
Winchcombe, Gloucestershire	SOUTH WEST
Windermere, Cumbria	NORTH WEST
Windsor, Berkshire	SOUTH EAST
Winster, Derbyshire	EAST MIDLANDS
Winterton-on-Sea, Norfolk	EAST
Wolverhampton, West Midlands	HEART OF ENGLAND
Woodbridge/Framlingham, Suffolk	EAST
Woodstock, Oxfordshire	SOUTH EAST
Wooler, Northumberland	NORTH EAST
Worcester, Worcestershire	HEART OF ENGLAND
Wroxham, Norfolk	EAST
Wymondham, Norfolk	EAST
Yelverton, Devon	SOUTH WEST
York, North Yorkshire	YORKSHIRE

© FHG Guides Ltd, 2013

ISBN 978-1-85055-456-1

Typeset by FHG Guides Ltd, Paisley.

Printed and bound in China by Imago.

Distribution. Book Trade: ORCA Book Services, Stanley House,
3 Fleets Lane, Poole, Dorset BH15 3AJ
(Tel: 01202 665432; Fax: 01202 666219)
e-mail: mail@orcabookservices.co.uk
Published by FHG Guides Ltd., Abbey Mill Business Centre,
Seedhill, Paisley PA1 ITJ (Tel: 0141-887 0428 Fax: 0141-889 7204).
e-mail: admin@fhguides.co.uk

750 Bed & Breakfasts in Britain is published by FHG Guides Ltd,
part of Kuperard Group.

Cover design: FHG Guides

Cover Picture: with thanks to

Double-Gate Farm, near Wells, Somerset (page 72)

Fisherman's Return, Winterton-on-Sea, Norfolk (page 116)